Healing the Inner Noise

Healing the Inner Noise

How to Quiet the Mind, Train Your Awareness, and Reclaim Mental Clarity

Lina Chaen

Mindful Pages

Published in 2025

ISBN: 9789374127483 (PB)
ISBN: 9789374129364 (eBook)

Published by

Mindful Pages
Imprint of Alpha Editions LLC
312 W. 2nd St #1834
Casper, WY 82601, USA

This book was developed using advanced writing tools to support the drafting and ideation process. All content has been thoughtfully curated, refined, and reviewed to ensure quality and relevance.

Content

Introduction
The Volume in Your Head

It often begins the moment we wake. Even before our eyes adjust to daylight, the commentary has started: the unfinished task, the remembered slight, the unresolved question looping like a refrain. By the time we reach for our phone, the mind is already ablaze with comparisons, worries, and half-formed decisions. For some, the chatter is a dull hum. For others, it is deafening. But for nearly everyone alive today, it is inescapable.

Consider the paradox: we live in an age of astonishing external quiet. Most of us are shielded from the primal dangers that haunted our ancestors—wild beasts, famine, tribal warfare—yet our minds remain restless, ceaselessly vigilant, perpetually scanning. This inner vigilance is the very trait that enabled us to survive as a species, yet in the conditions of modern life it becomes maladaptive, more torment than tool. The result is what I call the *volume in your head*—a relentless stream of thoughts, self-criticism, and "what-ifs" that neither resolve nor recede.

A statistic makes the point with unsettling clarity: neuroscientists estimate that we generate tens of thousands of thoughts each day, the majority of them repetitive. More striking still is how few of those thoughts provide fresh insight or direction. Most are echoes of yesterday's anxieties, projected into tomorrow. We may pride ourselves on being rational beings, yet the evidence suggests otherwise: the chatter is not under conscious control, and it is shaping our lives more than we dare to admit.

The Noise We Inherit

To understand this predicament, we must look backwards. For millennia, human survival depended upon a mind that anticipated danger before it arrived. The rustle in the grass might have been nothing—or it might have been a predator. The cautious ancestor, rehearsing possibilities and imagining threats, had better odds of survival than the reckless one. Mental noise, in this context, was an evolutionary masterpiece.

The problem is that we inhabit a world utterly unlike the one in which that mental system evolved. Our nervous systems are tuned to crises that rarely come, while the environment batters us with new forms of stimulation: breaking news alerts, emails that demand instant replies, a culture that equates busyness with worth. The same neural machinery that once scanned for predators now scans for notifications. The survival mechanism has become a saboteur.

Yet the noise is not merely a nuisance; it extracts a heavy toll. Psychologists have long documented the effects of chronic rumination: heightened anxiety, impaired decision-making, fatigue, and erosion of close relationships. Physicians trace its consequences into the body itself—elevated cortisol, disrupted sleep, inflammatory disease. Our mental static is not contained within the skull; it seeps into every corner of our lives.

The Ancient Discomfort with Silence

Across history, cultures have wrestled with this restlessness. Monastic traditions from East and West alike devised disciplines of silence to tame the mind's voice. Greek philosophers debated whether the soul could ever find tranquillity amidst worldly concerns. In more recent centuries, Romantic poets celebrated solitude while industrial modernity sought to eradicate it, replacing silence with productivity and the hum of machinery.

Today's discomfort with quiet has reached a fever pitch. In one well-known psychological experiment, participants were asked to sit alone in a silent room with nothing to occupy them but their thoughts. Many chose, instead, to administer small electric shocks to themselves. Better pain than stillness. The mind, untrained, rebels against silence.

This book argues that such rebellion is not evidence of weakness but proof of design. Our brains were built for vigilance, not for rest. Inner noise is the default setting, not a defect. The question is not how to rid ourselves of it, but how to understand it—how to train awareness so that we are no longer ruled by the voice in our heads but can guide it toward clarity, steadiness, even wisdom.

The Mind's Hidden Radio

Imagine, if you will, an old radio left on in the corner of a room. Static, snippets of speech, half-songs, interruptions—an endless stream of noise. For most of us, that is the soundtrack of consciousness: fragments of past and future, commentary without pause. We become so habituated to the hum that we mistake it for reality itself.

But the radio can be tuned. We can learn to distinguish between the signal and the noise, between thoughts worth heeding and those to be released. This tuning is not a mystical gift, nor a matter of sheer willpower. It draws upon skills now well-documented in psychology, neuroscience, and contemplative practice: metacognition, mindfulness, cognitive-behavioural techniques. At its core lies a simple but radical act: learning to watch the mind rather than be swept along by it.

This shift—from identification to observation—has profound consequences. Once we realise that the voice in our head is not the sum of who we are, but an inner narrator we can engage with, question, even rewrite, we reclaim an extraordinary measure of freedom. The chatter ceases to be the master; it becomes raw material for growth.

A Crisis of Attention

What makes this subject urgent now is not simply that inner noise has always plagued humanity. It is that modern life has turned the volume higher than ever before. The "attention economy" in which we live monetises distraction. Our devices are designed not merely to inform but to captivate, to trigger the very thought loops that evolution built into us. The result is a society where clarity is scarce, focus is fragile, and true stillness is rare.

This is more than an individual predicament. When leaders, policymakers, and educators are themselves ensnared in static, the consequences ripple outward. Poor decisions, reactive politics, frayed social bonds—these too are symptoms of unchecked mental noise. To quiet the chatter within is therefore not only a personal liberation but a cultural necessity.

What This Book Offers

Healing the Inner Noise invites you to engage with your mind in a new way. It does not promise an impossible silence, nor does it prescribe empty platitudes. Instead, it offers a framework for understanding the origins of mental chatter, recognising its patterns, and transforming its energy into clarity.

We will move from the evolutionary roots of restlessness to the cultural machines that amplify it, from the neuroscientific structures that generate loops of thought to the practical disciplines that interrupt them. Along the way, you will learn to meet the "inner narrator," to train attention as deliberately as one trains a muscle, to rewrite distorted stories, and to harness the body itself as an ally in mental calm.

The later chapters will extend these practices into daily life: relationships, work, leadership, creativity. The aim is not the sterile absence of thought but the emergence of a quieter, steadier mind—one in which noise no longer dictates, but instead serves as a background against which clarity, focus, and meaning can stand out.

The Questions Ahead

What if the inner noise we dread is not an enemy but a signal—clumsy, repetitive, yet filled with clues about our fears and values?
What if silence, rather than a void, is a form of intelligence

we have neglected?
What if the very act of attending to the mind's chatter could sharpen our awareness rather than drown it?

These are the questions that will guide us. They are not abstract. They touch every decision we make, every relationship we sustain, every hour of our waking life.

The promise of this book is not escape from noise but transformation of it. The mind will never cease to think, but it can learn to think differently—to move from static to music, from clamour to clarity. In learning this art, we do more than heal ourselves. We open the possibility of living, and leading, with a mind that is both audible and quiet: attuned, discerning, free.

And so we begin.

Chapter 1
The Mind's Hidden Radio

On a crowded commuter train, a woman sits still, her eyes fixed on the glass reflection in front of her. Outwardly, she is motionless. Inwardly, her mind is ablaze. She replays the awkward exchange with her manager from yesterday. She drafts and redrafts possible replies to an email she has not yet received. She calculates the time she will need to reach her next meeting, then imagines the embarrassment of arriving late. No one else on the train hears any of this. Yet to her, the noise is deafening.

This is the human condition: a mind that will not stop talking. Some days the voice is useful—alerting us to deadlines, guiding us through complex problems. On others, it is relentless, a barrage of "what ifs" and "if onlys" that leaves us anxious and depleted. We tell ourselves that we ought to be able to quiet it, that our failure to do so is a weakness. But what if the very opposite is true? What if the ceaseless chatter is not a flaw in our design, but proof of it?

The first task of this chapter is to name the paradox. We are the species that thinks about thinking. Our ancestors evolved minds that never rested, constantly scanning for threats and opportunities. This vigilance kept us alive. The ancestor who worried about whether the shadows concealed a predator had a better chance of surviving than the one who relaxed too easily. The mind's radio, always switched on, always searching for signal, was once a survival imperative.

Yet what once safeguarded our existence now often undermines it. The modern world rarely presents us with immediate physical danger. But the same mental system built for threat detection continues to broadcast, interpreting missed messages as threats to our reputation, delayed projects as existential hazards, ambiguous glances as evidence of rejection. We inherit an ancient mechanism operating on modern frequencies, and the result is a mind tuned to static.

To grasp the significance of this, it is crucial to distinguish between two modes of thought. On one hand, there is *thinking*—deliberate, structured, directed towards solving a problem or imagining a possibility. Thinking can be exhausting, but it is purposeful. On the other hand, there is *chatter*—circular, repetitive, untethered from resolution. Chatter is the voice that tells us the same story over and over again, long after it has served any use.

Most of us confuse the two. We imagine we are "working on" something when in fact we are circling it endlessly. The distinction is subtle but vital. Thinking adds to life. Chatter drains it. Learning to recognise when the mind has crossed this line is the beginning of freedom. It is like realising that the radio in the background is not a live conversation, but an old recording stuck on loop.

The cost of not noticing is immense. Psychologists catalogue it as anxiety, depression, decision fatigue. Physicians chart its progress in raised cortisol levels, poor sleep, inflammatory illness. But the toll is also relational and cultural. When we are caught in noise, we listen less well to those around us. We bring the same harsh inner critic into our interactions with others. Entire communities, workplaces, even societies can become locked into cycles of static, mistaking volume for vitality.

You need only glance at the culture around you to see this playing out: the constant refresh of news feeds, the addictive pull of notifications, the way we equate being busy with being important. The result is a civilisation whose collective mind is perpetually unsettled, a shared atmosphere of mental noise. Each individual struggle is amplified by the cultural echo chamber.

And yet—this is where the story takes its surprising turn. For the very system that overwhelms us is also the source of our greatest capacities. That same inner radio that replays our fears is also the one that rehearses our future achievements. The same imagination that tortures us with "what if" also allows us to create art, to build societies, to care about people we have never met. Inner noise, unrefined, sabotages. But inner noise, recognised and trained, becomes raw material for awareness, resilience, even creativity.

This chapter will explore that tension. We will examine why we cannot stop thinking, and why this is not a failure but an inheritance. We will learn how to distinguish between useful thought and unproductive chatter, and why making this distinction matters so urgently. We will face the costs of unchecked noise, not only in personal terms but in the wider culture we share. And finally, we will glimpse the hidden opportunity: how the very chatter that burdens us can, with skill and practice, become a wellspring of clarity.

The radio in your head will never fall completely silent. But it need not dominate the room. The pages ahead are an invitation to step closer to the dial, to understand its workings, and to discover that beneath the static lies a signal worth hearing.

Why We Can't Stop Thinking

At three o'clock in the morning, long after the world outside has fallen silent, the mind refuses to rest. It revisits the day's unfinished conversations, replays mistakes from years ago, or spins out scenarios that will never happen. Few things feel lonelier than lying awake, watching the ceiling in darkness, while thought after thought parades unbidden. We call it overthinking, as if it were a defect of character. Yet this restless mental energy is not a weakness at all. It is the natural outcome of how human cognition evolved: a mind that, to keep us alive, never stopped scanning the horizon.

Our ancestors were not burdened by board meetings or unanswered emails, but they faced threats far more immediate. The crack of a branch in the forest, the shadow moving at the edge of firelight—these could mean the difference between life and death. The nervous system that paused to imagine danger, that rehearsed escape routes before they were needed, was a system more likely to survive. Thinking was vigilance. Over-preparation was a kind of insurance policy. And so natural selection favoured the restless mind.

The mind we inherit today is that same survival instrument. It runs on ancient programming: detect a threat, imagine the worst, rehearse every possibility. What has changed is the environment. The dangers of the savannah have been replaced by performance reviews, mortgage payments, and the ceaseless feed of digital news. The mechanism itself has not evolved at the same pace as culture. The result is that we carry a Stone Age brain in a smartphone age, endlessly applying protective habits to situations that rarely require them. The mismatch is profound—and exhausting.

This helps explain the paradox at the heart of our thinking. We imagine thought as something we *do*, an intentional act of reasoning. In truth, much of what occupies the mind is automatic. Neuroscience has shown that even at rest, when we are not focused on a task, the brain's "default mode network" whirs into action. It generates daydreams, replays, and speculative futures. In evolutionary terms, this was adaptive: better to anticipate danger than be surprised by it. But in modern life, the same process means we spend hours rehearsing conversations that never take place or predicting disasters that never arrive.

The irony is that this mental activity often feels purposeful in the moment. We believe we are solving problems when we are, in fact, circling them endlessly. Productive thinking leads somewhere; it builds bridges between ideas or guides us to action. Chatter does not. It repeats, it intensifies, it narrows the field of vision until nothing exists but the loop itself. Anyone who has lain awake revisiting a single embarrassing moment knows the futility of it. Yet still the cycle continues, because the brain is not designed to give up until every angle has been explored.

One might ask: why doesn't the mind simply quieten once danger has passed? The answer lies in its asymmetry. Missing a genuine threat could be fatal, while imagining one that never materialises costs little. Evolution therefore erred on the side of caution, privileging false alarms over missed signals. This is why anxiety, though unpleasant, is such a common human experience. It is not a malfunction; it is the mind's way of over-delivering on its protective mandate.

But the cost, in contemporary life, is real. Psychologists warn that chronic overthinking depletes working memory, leaving us less capable of focus and decision-making. Doctors trace its effects into the body: elevated stress hormones, cardiovascular strain, immune suppression. Relationships suffer too. When the mind is preoccupied with imagined conversations, it listens less to the real voices beside us. The very mechanism meant to keep us safe begins to corrode the quality of our days.

This toll is not merely personal; it is cultural. Societies that valorise constant activity and perpetual vigilance reinforce the mind's natural restlessness. The workplace that rewards employees for being "always on" aligns perfectly with the brain's bias towards scanning and worrying. Social media amplifies this by offering a continuous stream of signals, each one hinting at danger, opportunity, or exclusion. We are caught in an echo chamber of vigilance, our ancient survival system manipulated by modern design.

And yet, there is another side to this story. The mind that anticipates threats is also the mind that imagines possibilities. The same neural circuits that replay past mistakes are those that project future achievements. Our creativity, our moral imagination, our ability to plan and innovate—these too are products of the restless brain. Without the capacity to simulate scenarios, there would be no science, no art, no culture worth inheriting. What we call overthinking is not a different mechanism from creativity; it is the same mechanism, misapplied.

This perspective changes how we approach the problem. If we treat inner noise as a defect, our only strategy is suppression—an effort doomed to fail, since the brain is built to generate thought. If we treat it instead as raw material, we can learn to redirect it. The goal is not to stop thinking but to distinguish between chatter and useful cognition, to step back from the loop and choose where to place attention.

Consider the radio once more. Left untuned, it produces static. But in the same frequencies lie music and meaning. The task is not to silence the broadcast but to refine our listening. Overthinking becomes less a trap than an opportunity: the chance to notice patterns, to learn where our fears cluster, to see what the mind believes is most urgent. Awareness transforms noise into signal.

Perhaps the real challenge is not why we cannot stop thinking, but whether we can learn to live wisely with the stream of thought that never ceases. What would it mean to treat the restless mind not as a tyrant to be overthrown, but as an ally to be trained? Could we accept that the very system that wakes us at three in the morning is also the one that allows us to write poetry, fall in love, or plan for a future that does not yet exist?

The brain's hidden radio will not switch off. But it can be tuned. The deeper question—the one that lingers as you turn the page—is how to discern the difference between protective vigilance and destructive chatter, and how to reclaim authority over the volume in your head without silencing the remarkable instrument itself.

The Difference Between Thinking and Chatter

Thomas Edison was once asked how he had managed to create the light bulb after so many failed attempts. His response was sharp: "I have not failed. I've just found 10,000 ways that won't work." Whatever one makes of Edison's bravado, his remark captures the essence of *thinking*: a structured engagement with problems, a process that, even in apparent failure, moves forward. Contrast this with the sleepless night of someone obsessively replaying an awkward exchange at a dinner party, revisiting the same words a hundred times without fresh insight. That is *chatter*: repetitive, unproductive, and corrosive. Both arise from the same machinery of mind. Yet one is a tool; the other, a trap.

The paradox is that chatter often disguises itself as thinking. It feels like effort. It can even mimic problem-solving, at least at first. A lawyer turning a case over in her mind late into the night believes she is preparing. An athlete revisiting a lost game thinks he is analysing. But beyond a certain point, the process ceases to yield progress. The same loops return. Energy is spent, but nothing is gained. The distinction between thinking and chatter is not always obvious in the moment, but learning to detect it is crucial if we are to reclaim authority over our mental lives.

Thinking, at its core, is purposeful. It is the deliberate manipulation of ideas in service of a goal: to solve a problem, to weigh options, to anticipate consequences. Cognitive scientists describe it as a form of "mental work," and like all work, it has direction and an endpoint. You think about a route to avoid traffic, and you arrive at a decision. You think through a strategy, and you draft a plan. Productive thought clarifies, guides, and, in its best form, expands the horizon of what is possible.

Chatter is directionless. It loops without resolution. Instead of clarifying, it clouds. Instead of opening possibilities, it narrows them. The more we rehearse the same mental script, the more it entrenches itself. A single worry grows into a conviction. A minor misstep hardens into a story of personal inadequacy. In chatter, the mind mistakes motion for progress. Like a treadmill, it expends enormous energy but arrives nowhere new.

This distinction is not merely semantic. Neuroscientific research suggests that different brain networks are implicated. Productive problem-solving recruits the prefrontal cortex, the region associated with executive control and decision-making. Rumination, by contrast, is driven largely by the default mode network, which generates self-referential narratives and replays. In other words, thinking draws on the circuits that direct action; chatter is what happens when the brain is left to recycle its own content without oversight.

Philosophers have long recognised this difference. The Stoics warned against becoming prisoners of mental rehearsal, urging instead a disciplined focus on what lies within one's control. Descartes, for all his emphasis on methodical doubt, insisted that thought should be ordered and purposeful, not a cascade of unchecked impressions. Even Eastern traditions, from Buddhist meditation to Taoist writings, distinguished between the mind's useful capacities and its tendency to entangle itself in needless loops. Across cultures, the recognition is consistent: not all thinking is equal, and unchecked chatter is a source of suffering.

Modern psychology puts the matter more starkly. Productive thought correlates with resilience and creativity. Rumination correlates with anxiety, depression, and impaired performance. A manager facing a complex decision benefits from careful reflection; the same manager paralysed by indecision, replaying worst-case scenarios, suffers the cost of chatter. The shift from one state to the other can be subtle—a matter of minutes or even seconds—but the consequences diverge dramatically.

So how can we tell the difference? The most practical clue lies in whether the process moves forward or circles back. Productive thinking generates new connections, possible actions, or at least a clearer understanding. Chatter simply restates the same content with mounting emotional charge. Ask yourself: *Is this line of thought producing options I could act upon? Or am I merely repeating what I already know?* The first is thinking. The second is chatter.

Another sign is the body. Productive thinking may be effortful, but it does not usually hijack physiology. Chatter, by contrast, often recruits the stress response: a quickened heartbeat, tense muscles, shallow breath. The body signals that the mind has tipped from analysis into fixation. These cues are not always dramatic, but they are reliable indicators that the line has been crossed.

Context matters too. A scientist who spends hours exploring a question in the lab is engaged in rigorous thinking. The same scientist, at home, unable to let go of a minor oversight, may fall into chatter. The mind's capacity to apply itself effectively is not unlimited. When fatigued, anxious, or lacking perspective, its natural inclination is to default to loops rather than breakthroughs. Recognising this is less an indictment than a reminder: the difference between thinking and chatter is not one of capacity, but of state.

Importantly, chatter often carries an illusion of necessity. It whispers: *If I keep replaying this, I will find a solution.* This illusion is powerful precisely because the mind evolved to solve problems. But the truth is that the solutions chatter promises rarely arrive. Instead, it depletes the very resources needed for genuine thinking. Decision fatigue, attention overload, and emotional exhaustion follow. The ancient survival mechanism—over-preparing for threats—runs overtime, sabotaging the clarity it was designed to protect.

This is why the framework matters. If we can notice the shift, we can interrupt it. To say "this is chatter" is already to loosen its grip. Naming creates distance. From there, we can choose whether to redirect our attention, externalise the thought through writing, or simply pause. The point is not to suppress the mind's activity, but to reclaim the power to discern which activity serves us and which drains us.

Seen in this light, the difference between thinking and chatter is not just academic. It is existential. The quality of our inner life depends on which mode predominates. A culture that confuses constant mental busyness with productivity risks enshrining chatter as virtue, leaving less room for deep thought. An individual who cannot tell the difference risks exhausting themselves on loops that masquerade as work but deliver only stress.

The open question, then, is this: can we, in the midst of modern overstimulation, learn to make this distinction habitually? Can we cultivate the sensitivity to know when the mind is generating possibilities and when it is merely repeating itself? The answer may determine not only our personal clarity, but also our collective capacity to think wisely in a world already too noisy.

The Cost of Inner Noise

A surgeon stands over the operating table, scalpel in hand, yet his attention drifts. A fragment of last night's argument returns uninvited; a worry about his mortgage presses at the edges of thought. The noise is invisible to those around him, but it is there all the same—interfering, distracting, corroding his focus. Multiply this by millions of people in ordinary roles—teachers, drivers, parents, executives—and a picture emerges of how inner noise exacts its toll. What seems like a private burden turns out to be a shared condition with consequences both intimate and cultural.

The paradox is striking. The mind is our most powerful resource, yet its incessant chatter often undermines the very clarity it was designed to protect. Left unchecked, inner noise wears down attention, heightens stress, and drains emotional energy. It is not merely a nuisance; it is a tax on every decision, every relationship, every moment of potential rest. Understanding its cost is essential if we are to reclaim authority over it.

Psychologically, the most immediate effect of mental chatter is heightened stress. The brain's stress system does not discriminate between an actual threat and an imagined one. When thoughts replay possible disasters—What if I lose my job? What if they reject me?—the body reacts as though danger is imminent. Cortisol rises, heart rate accelerates, muscles tighten. Short bursts of this response are adaptive; they prime us for action. But when chatter sustains the alarm long after the moment has passed, the system becomes corrosive. Chronic stress reshapes the brain itself, reinforcing the very circuits that generate more rumination. It is a vicious loop: worry triggers stress, which sharpens worry.

Beyond stress lies decision fatigue. Modern life demands constant choices: which email to answer first, what to eat for dinner, how to allocate time between work and family. Each decision requires mental energy, and chatter siphons that energy away. Studies in cognitive psychology show that people with high levels of rumination perform worse on tasks requiring executive control. Their bandwidth is already consumed by internal rehearsal, leaving less capacity for deliberate reasoning. What looks like procrastination or indecision is often the by-product of noise exhausting the mind's decision-making system before the real work begins.

The toll extends further still into relationships. Chatter narrows perspective. When caught in cycles of self-critical thought, people listen less well, misinterpret neutral comments as hostile, and project their own anxieties onto others. A spouse distracted by mental replay may miss subtle cues of affection. A manager absorbed in private worry may fail to notice an employee's unspoken distress.

The inner voice, once it grows too loud, drowns out the outer world. Disconnection follows—not because people do not care, but because they cannot hear clearly through the static of their own minds.

It would be tempting to treat these as isolated personal struggles, but the reality is cultural amplification. Ours is a society that rewards hyper-vigilance. The always-on workplace, the 24-hour news cycle, the constant ping of notifications—each colludes with the mind's natural restlessness to produce an environment of perpetual overload. What once evolved as a survival system is now monetised. Social media thrives on comparison and anxiety, fuelling thought loops of inadequacy. News outlets compete for attention with headlines that keep the brain scanning for threat. We live in a marketplace that profits from our inability to switch off.

This has profound implications. At scale, a population caught in cycles of chatter is more anxious, less decisive, more prone to polarisation. Public discourse itself becomes noisy—filled with quick reactions rather than measured reflection. The same forces that erode individual focus also weaken collective clarity. A culture dominated by inner noise cannot deliberate well, cannot rest deeply, cannot easily sustain trust. The costs are not confined to the psyche; they ripple into politics, economics, and community life.

Yet it is important to note that not all inner noise is equally destructive. A student rehearsing exam material is not doomed to burnout; a parent replaying a conversation with their child may arrive at genuine insight. The problem arises when the process becomes compulsive, repetitive, detached from resolution. Productive thought has an arc: beginning, middle, end. Chatter is endless middle—motion without progress. The cost is not only wasted time but wasted vitality. The mind, fatigued by loops, has less to give to creativity, to empathy, to joy.

Consider sleep, one of the most fundamental human needs. Inner noise is a primary culprit in insomnia. The day's unresolved chatter carries into the night, denying the brain the rest required to consolidate memory, regulate emotion, and restore the body. A sleepless night due to racing thoughts is not a minor inconvenience; it is a physiological blow whose effects reverberate through attention, immunity, and mood. Multiply this across weeks and years, and the long-term cost becomes evident: a body less resilient, a mind less clear, a life less lived.

To appreciate the true burden of mental chatter is not to indulge in despair but to name reality with precision. We are not weak because we worry. We are not broken because we ruminate. We are inheritors of a survival system that, when unchecked, over-functions. The costs—psychological stress, decision fatigue, relational disconnection, cultural overload—are the price of letting the volume run high without intervention.

The open question is whether we can learn to interrupt this cycle before the toll becomes too steep. Can we, as individuals and as societies, create conditions in which thought retains its vitality without descending into endless noise? Can we recover the possibility of attention, connection, and rest in a culture that thrives on distraction?

The costs of inner noise are heavy. Yet to measure them clearly is to begin to imagine alternatives. The mind will never cease its broadcasting, but perhaps we can learn to step back, tune wisely, and decide which signals deserve to be amplified—and which are best allowed to fade into quiet.

The Hidden Opportunity

In 1816, the poet Lord Byron described his own mind as a storm: relentless thoughts, restless energy, a constant struggle to find peace. Yet from that turbulence emerged works of astonishing beauty. His inner noise, corrosive at times, also fuelled creativity that outlived him by centuries. This paradox—distress entangled with brilliance—raises a provocative question: what if the chatter we try so hard to silence is also a source of strength, provided we learn to work with it rather than against it?

For most of us, inner noise feels like sabotage. It distracts, unsettles, and exhausts. But beneath its surface lies a different possibility. The same mechanisms that produce worry also sharpen foresight. The same tendencies that replay past mistakes also enable reflection and learning. What we call mental static is not inert interference; it is raw material. With discernment, it can be shaped into insight, resilience, even creativity. The problem is not that the mind produces too much. The problem is that we have not yet mastered how to harness what it produces.

Psychologists studying creativity often note the importance of divergent thinking—the ability to generate multiple possibilities, to let the mind wander into unexpected territory. Left uncontrolled, this can become rumination. But directed with skill, it becomes the seedbed of innovation. Consider the breakthroughs of scientists who described solutions arriving not during periods of intense focus but in moments of distraction: Kekulé dreaming of a snake biting its tail and realising the structure of benzene; Einstein imagining himself riding on a beam of light. These are not accidents of silence but transformations of noise. What appeared as idle wandering became a channel for discovery.

There is also resilience hidden in the loops. The over-prepared mind, constantly rehearsing dangers, often creates buffers against shock. Those who have imagined the worst-case scenario are not paralysed when difficulty arrives; they are ready. Studies of soldiers and first responders suggest that controlled mental rehearsal—even of catastrophic scenarios—can build psychological armour. The very patterns that torment us in everyday life can, when reframed, prepare us to endure real crises with greater steadiness. The chatter becomes training, like a sparring partner who pushes us to strengthen muscles we might not otherwise use.

At the personal level, inner noise can be a mirror. The mind does not replay everything equally; it circles what matters most. A professional who cannot stop thinking about a neglected project may be hearing the signal of unrealised ambition. A parent obsessing over a child's wellbeing may be confronting the depth of their attachment. In this sense, the content of chatter is not random static but a crude index of values. By paying attention—not to every word, but to the patterns—we can discern where our energies and loyalties truly lie. The loops reveal us to ourselves.

This is not to romanticise suffering. Rumination unchecked is damaging, as already explored. But the challenge is to extract meaning from the noise without being drowned by it. One way is through deliberate externalisation: writing down recurring thoughts. Research on expressive writing shows that articulating worries in concrete form can transform amorphous noise into structured narrative, reducing emotional burden and opening space for perspective. The chatter, once caged on the page, can be studied, questioned, reframed. What was once sabotage becomes a resource for clarity.

Philosophically, the hidden opportunity of inner noise challenges our modern obsession with efficiency. We tend to treat every mental state as useful only if it leads directly to output. But some of the richest human experiences—reflection, imagination, creativity—emerge from the seemingly inefficient. To wish away inner noise entirely is to wish away the conditions under which much of culture, art, and moral progress have arisen. The mind's restlessness, properly guided, is not an obstacle to flourishing but one of its engines.

Culturally, this reframe is urgent. We inhabit a world that pathologises almost any departure from productivity. The employee distracted by daydreams is labelled unproductive. The student staring out the window is said to be wasting time. Yet history is filled with innovations born from precisely these moments. The suppression of inner wandering risks cutting us off from the very creativity needed to solve collective problems. If we view mental chatter solely as noise, we impoverish ourselves. If we see it as potential, we expand the scope of human possibility.

The challenge, then, is not to silence the radio but to become better listeners. What is this thought loop trying to signal? What possibility is embedded in this restless rehearsal? Can the same energy that generates fear be channelled into preparation, invention, or deeper understanding of self? These questions turn inner noise from adversary to ally.

But here lies the tension. For every Byron whose turbulence produced lasting art, there are countless lives frayed by loops that never resolve. The difference is not the presence of noise but the capacity to harness it. And that capacity is not innate; it is learned, trained, cultivated. The mind's chatter will never disappear. The choice is whether to remain captive to it—or to transform it into a resource that sharpens awareness and enriches life.

What if, instead of fearing the mind's endless voice, we learned to ask what it might be offering? Could we discover, in the very thing that unsettles us, the outlines of our deepest insights and strengths? The noise will always be there. The opportunity is whether we will continue to treat it as interference—or finally recognise it as the signal we have been waiting to hear.

Chapter 2
The Roots of Restlessness

In 1953, an American psychologist named Jerome Kagan placed infants in a laboratory setting and introduced them to unfamiliar objects, noises, and faces. Some babies remained calm, gazing with curiosity. Others reacted with visible agitation—crying, stiffening, their bodies signalling distress before any real threat was present. Kagan's research would help establish a principle both ancient and urgent: the human mind is wired not simply to respond to danger, but to anticipate it. The infant's alarm, like the adult's restless worry, was not about what *was* but about what *might be*. From the very beginning, our inner lives have been tuned towards vigilance.

This capacity for foresight is, on the face of it, a triumph. It allows us to plan, to imagine futures, to prepare for crises before they arrive. Civilisations were built on such anticipation: crops planted against famine, shelters designed for storms, legal systems devised to ward off chaos. Yet the gift carries its own curse. The same imagination that prepares us for tomorrow also burdens us with scenarios that never materialise. We suffer twice—first in imagination, then, if misfortune strikes, in reality. Evolution gave us foresight, but in doing so, it bequeathed us worry.

To appreciate how this inheritance shapes modern life, one need only glance at the devices that rarely leave our hands.

The survival instinct that once scanned the forest edge now scans newsfeeds. Where our ancestors listened for the predator's rustle, we listen for the next notification. The difference is scale. A rustle in the grass happened occasionally; our phones rustle every few minutes. The vigilance that once protected us is now endlessly triggered, amplified into a condition of permanent distraction. What was adaptive in the savannah has become exhausting in the office, the classroom, the home.

The media environment intensifies this still further. Twenty-four-hour news cycles thrive on fear, because fear guarantees attention. Social media, with its relentless comparisons, stokes insecurities that keep the mind rehearsing its inadequacies. The result is a society in which the brain's ancient alert system is constantly overfed. We are not failing when we feel restless; we are living in conditions designed to keep us that way.

But human restlessness is not solely a story of biology and technology. It is also cultural. For centuries, societies have differed in their attitudes towards silence. Monastic traditions in Buddhism and Christianity treated silence as a discipline, a gateway to clarity. Ancient Stoics spoke of tranquillity as the highest achievement of reason. By contrast, modern hustle culture treats silence with suspicion. Idleness is seen as weakness, stillness as wasted opportunity. In the language of productivity, every quiet moment must be filled with output, lest it be judged unworthy.

This suspicion of quiet is more revealing than it seems. It suggests that beneath our craving for peace lies a fear of what we might encounter there. Left alone with our thoughts, many of us feel unease, even dread. Psychologists have confirmed this in experiments where people, asked to sit in silence without stimulation, often prefer to administer small electric shocks to themselves rather than endure stillness. Restlessness is not simply imposed from outside; it arises also from within, a discomfort with silence itself.

The roots of this tension run deep. On the one hand, we long for calm. On the other, we equate stillness with boredom, with lack of control, even with mortality. Silence reminds us that we are finite creatures, vulnerable and unoccupied. To drown it out with noise—whether external or internal—is to distract ourselves from that confrontation. Thus we oscillate, craving the very thing we resist.

This chapter will trace these roots with care: the double-edged gift of evolution, the technological machinery that exploits it, the cultural habits that shape our attitude to quiet, and the psychological paradox that keeps us afraid of the very stillness we desire. To understand restlessness is to see not only why we think as we do, but why societies are built as they are.

The question that follows is simple yet unsettling: if restlessness is both inheritance and habit, biological and cultural, can it be unlearned—or is it the permanent condition of the human mind? The search for that answer begins here.

Evolution's Double-Edged Gift

On a quiet plain some 200,000 years ago, a small band of humans paused at dusk. For most, the day's labour was over. But one, crouching near the fire, remained tense, eyes scanning the tall grass. He could not relax. He imagined predators lurking where shadows deepened. His companions might have teased him for his unease, yet when danger did arrive—when a lion emerged from the brush—it was his vigilance that bought them precious seconds. That ancient habit of anticipating what might go wrong helped his kin survive, and by extension, shaped the very inheritance of our minds today.

This is the paradox of human cognition: the same foresight that enabled us to build cities, chart oceans, and launch satellites also burdens us with worry, rumination, and insomnia. We are creatures uniquely able to see beyond the present, but this gift is inseparable from the costs of imagining too much. To understand our restlessness, we must first reckon with this evolutionary trade-off: the mind designed to anticipate threat is also the mind condemned to generate loops of anxiety.

From the standpoint of survival, the asymmetry was clear. To mistake a rustle in the grass for a predator when it was only the wind cost little; to dismiss it when it was a lion could mean death. Our ancestors survived not by accuracy but by excess caution. Evolution thus weighted the mind towards false alarms, privileging vigilance over tranquillity. The cognitive system we inherit is biased by design: it rehearses dangers, scans relentlessly, and errs on the side of worry.

Anthropologists have traced this vigilance to a suite of adaptive traits: hyperactive threat detection, predictive modelling of the future, and the ability to mentally time-travel. These features allowed humans to plan migrations, anticipate drought, and avoid hostile encounters. But they also laid the foundation for what modern psychology calls *rumination*. The very machinery that scans the environment outwardly can, in the absence of immediate threat, turn inward, re-examining past failures and projecting imagined futures. The predator no longer has to be real; it can live entirely in thought.

Consider the role of memory. Unlike most animals, humans do not merely recall; we reconstruct. The act of remembering is entangled with imagining, so every recollection carries us forward as well as backward. This capacity gave us foresight, but it also meant that past pain could be re-experienced indefinitely. The hunter who nearly starved during a lean season remembered not only the fact of hunger but its sensations, and those memories amplified future vigilance. Today, the same mechanism ensures we relive humiliations long after the event, or anticipate conversations that never take place. What was once insurance has become over-insurance, saturating our lives with imagined rehearsals.

Neuroscience has begun to map this terrain. The *default mode network,* active when the brain is not engaged in external tasks, generates spontaneous thought: daydreams, recollections, projections. Functional MRI studies show that this network lights up precisely when people are caught in loops of self-reflection, worry, or fantasy. It is the neural echo of our evolutionary history, evidence that the mind's resting state is not rest at all but vigilance by other means. What we call "quiet" is often only an unstructured flood of thoughts.

Yet the double-edged nature of this gift becomes clearer when we note its achievements. The same capacity to imagine misfortune is what allows us to plan defences against it. The mental rehearsal of disaster spurred the invention of tools, rituals, and collective strategies. Fear of famine led to agriculture; fear of invasion led to alliances. The uneasy anticipation of "what if" drove ingenuity as much as it fuelled anxiety. Even today, entrepreneurs and scientists draw upon this foresight: anticipating risks, troubleshooting before they arise, playing out scenarios that others overlook. What seems like worry can, under discipline, become vision.

Still, the cost is heavy when the rehearsal is endless. Unlike our ancestors, we are rarely able to discharge the energy of vigilance through immediate action. The predator does not come; the famine never arrives. Yet the body has already prepared: adrenaline surges, cortisol floods, the heart races. Chronic activation of these systems undermines health, producing anxiety disorders, hypertension, and fatigue. The survival gift, misapplied, corrodes the very life it was meant to protect.

Philosophers have long recognised this tension. Seneca observed that "we suffer more in imagination than in reality." The Buddha diagnosed restless craving and fear as the sources of human dissatisfaction. In different vocabularies, both pointed to the same condition: a mind that cannot stop anticipating, a gift that becomes a torment. What is striking is how consistent this observation is across cultures and centuries. The double edge of foresight is not a modern predicament but the human predicament.

And yet, it would be misleading to suggest that the solution lies in stripping foresight away. Without it, we would lose much of what makes us human: the ability to plan across generations, to imagine futures not yet lived, to weigh not only immediate gain but long-term consequence. The challenge is not to undo evolution but to become more skilful custodians of its legacy. To learn when vigilance serves us and when it ensnares us.

Perhaps the most pressing question, then, is this: can we harness the same neural machinery that produces worry to cultivate clarity instead? If foresight is both our triumph and our torment, is it possible to train the mind to retain the gift without succumbing to its cost? Evolution gave us a double-edged blade. How we hold it—and whether we learn to cut with precision rather than wound ourselves—remains unresolved.

The Modern Noise Machine

In 2007, when Apple unveiled the first iPhone, the device was hailed as a miracle of design—an elegant pocket computer that promised freedom, efficiency, and endless connection. Few foresaw that in little more than a decade, the glow of its screen would become one of the most dominant features of modern life. Today, the average person checks their phone hundreds of times a day. What began as a tool for convenience has evolved into something closer to compulsion. We are living inside a vast machine that monetises distraction, one that does not simply respond to our cognitive habits but amplifies them into a condition of near-permanent noise.

The irony is profound. Evolution gave us minds that scan the environment for threat and opportunity, rarely satisfied with the present moment. Technology has learned to exploit that restlessness, feeding it with endless prompts, updates, and alerts. The survival mechanism that once helped us notice the rustle of a predator in the bushes is now hooked by the ping of a notification. What once preserved our species now keeps us scrolling long past midnight, half-engaged, half-anxious, and rarely at rest.

Consider the news cycle. In earlier centuries, news arrived in measured doses: a daily broadsheet, a weekly gazette, a town crier with selective announcements. Now it flows in torrents, twenty-four hours a day, across multiple platforms, each competing for attention. The logic is simple: fear, outrage, and urgency command clicks. Stories are written to keep our vigilance circuits activated, to ensure we return for more. This is not conspiracy but economics. Attention has become currency, and fear is the most reliable way to secure it. The result is a public perpetually on edge, immersed in a narrative of crises that never end.

Social media adds a different, though related, layer. Where the news appeals to our instinct for threat detection, social platforms target our need for belonging and status. Each notification is a potential signal of inclusion or exclusion: a like, a share, a comment. The brain, attuned to social survival as much as physical, cannot easily ignore these cues. Anthropologists remind us that in small groups, social rejection once meant literal danger—loss of protection, food, or mates. Today, no physical peril follows a lack of digital approval, yet the same circuits fire, keeping us tethered to the feed.

What makes the modern noise machine particularly insidious is its portability. Unlike the lion on the savannah, which appeared only occasionally, our predators are in our pockets, always within reach. The result is *ambient distraction*—not the dramatic interruption of a single crisis but the slow erosion of attention through constant micro-stimuli. Each time we check a screen, the brain receives a small jolt of novelty, a hit of dopamine. Over time, we become conditioned to crave it, to feel restless without it. The silence that once allowed thoughts to settle is now crowded out by flickering updates, each insignificant on its own but overwhelming in accumulation.

The cultural consequences are visible. Workplaces demand continuous responsiveness, blurring the boundary between professional and personal life. Leisure, once defined by rest, is colonised by devices that deliver entertainment but deny stillness. Even intimate conversations are punctuated by glances at glowing screens, fragments of attention siphoned away. The noise is no longer confined to the mind; it saturates the environment, shaping how we live together as much as how we think alone.

Yet there is another layer to the story: the machine is not merely external. Technology did not invent our restlessness; it exploits it. The constant checking, the inability to resist the scroll, the fear of missing out—these are not entirely new. They are extensions of ancient habits: vigilance for danger, sensitivity to social standing, hunger for novelty. What is new is the scale and intensity. The modern noise machine industrialises these instincts, feeding them with precision, ensuring they are never sated.

Some defend this as progress. Access to limitless information, connection across distance, and opportunities for self-expression are indeed remarkable achievements. A farmer in rural India can learn global market prices instantly; a teenager in Brazil can share art with peers in

Seoul; a doctor can consult medical research in real time. These are profound goods. But they come with a hidden cost: the erosion of depth. When attention is fragmented into constant microbursts, the mind loses its capacity for sustained thought, and the chatter within is amplified rather than calmed.

Philosophically, the modern noise machine raises unsettling questions about autonomy. If our most ancient instincts can be manipulated so effortlessly, what does it mean to exercise choice? Are we, as individuals, still the authors of our attention, or have we ceded that role to algorithms designed to capture and monetise it? The noise in our heads is no longer entirely ours; it is curated, nudged, shaped by forces that profit from our distraction.

And yet, the machine is not invincible. Awareness of its mechanics is the first step towards reclaiming agency. Just as our ancestors learned to control fire—once both a danger and a gift—we may learn to control the blaze of digital distraction. The capacity for foresight, though exploited, remains ours to direct. But it requires effort: deliberate practices of silence, intentional boundaries, conscious refusals.

The deeper question lingers: if the noise is now woven into the fabric of modern life, can it truly be quieted, or must we learn instead to navigate it differently? Perhaps the task is not to dismantle the machine but to outwit it—to recover spaces where attention can rest, even within a culture designed to keep it restless. The survival system we inherited has been hijacked by the tools we created. Whether we can reclaim it, or whether we will live permanently tuned to the static, remains unresolved.

Culture and Silence

In 2014, psychologists at the University of Virginia conducted a simple but startling experiment. Participants were asked to sit quietly in an empty room for fifteen minutes, with nothing to do but be alone with their thoughts. Many reported the experience as unpleasant. Some went so far as to press a button that delivered small electric shocks, preferring pain over silence. The study revealed something unsettling about modern life: we crave quiet in theory, yet in practice we find it unbearable. Why should silence, once revered as sacred in so many cultures, now feel intolerable to so many of us?

The answer is not uniform across societies or eras. Silence has carried profoundly different meanings depending on context. For Buddhist monks in Southeast Asia, silence is cultivated as a discipline, the ground of insight and liberation. In the Japanese aesthetic of *ma,* silence and space are treated not as absence but as active presences that give shape to experience. Medieval Christian monasteries imposed vows of silence not merely to repress speech but to redirect attention inward, towards God. In these traditions, quiet was not a void to be filled but a vessel to be entered—a necessary condition for depth.

Contrast this with the modern West, where silence is often equated with awkwardness or deficiency. In the office, a lull in conversation can feel like failure; in the home, background noise from television or radio is left running to fill the air. Hustle culture has only deepened this aversion. Productivity manuals praise the art of "optimising every minute," leaving little room for stillness. A quiet hour is not framed as replenishment but as wasted opportunity. To pause is to risk being outpaced. In this cultural climate, silence becomes suspect, as if it signals laziness, incompetence, or loss of relevance.

Anthropologists suggest that attitudes towards silence reveal underlying values about selfhood and community. In societies that emphasise collectivism, such as many Indigenous traditions, silence can function as respect—listening more than speaking, allowing space for others to be heard. In contrast, in cultures that prize assertive individualism, silence is often treated as weakness or invisibility. The Scandinavian concept of *tystnadskultur* (the "culture of silence") reflects norms of restraint and modesty, where speaking too much is frowned upon. Meanwhile, in North America, conversational gaps are often rushed to be filled, as if to leave them open would be to abandon connection.

This divergence highlights a key tension: silence is not a universal experience but a cultural construct. What feels peaceful in one setting can feel oppressive in another. A Buddhist monk's silence is liberation; a corporate employee's silence in a meeting can be career suicide. Our discomfort with quiet is not merely psychological; it is shaped by social expectations about what it means to participate, to contribute, to belong.

Technology has intensified this cultural divide. With smartphones in our pockets, silence has become optional in a way it never was before. Every gap in conversation, every pause at a bus stop, every moment alone can be filled with music, podcasts, or endless scrolling. The possibility of uninterrupted stillness has been replaced by the compulsion to fill time. What older traditions cultivated as a practice of depth, modern culture interrupts with an infinite feed of surface. We now face the peculiar condition of being surrounded by noise not because we lack silence but because we fear what silence might reveal.

At its heart, this fear is existential. Silence confronts us with the raw material of our own minds: the chatter, the doubts, the desires we work so hard to outrun. It exposes the difference between who we imagine ourselves to be and who we actually are when stripped of distraction. No wonder so many flinch. To sit quietly is to come face-to-face with the fact of our own interiority, and by extension, our own mortality. For some traditions, this confrontation was the gateway to wisdom. For us, it is often the signal to reach for a device.

Yet silence retains its power, even in a noisy age. Writers retreat to cabins, executives to silent retreats, artists to remote residencies. Patients recovering from trauma often describe silence as a precondition for healing. Neuroscientific studies suggest that periods of quiet allow the brain to integrate memory and emotion, clearing space for creativity and resilience. Silence, in this sense, is not a luxury but a physiological necessity. The irony is that the very thing we resist is the thing we most need.

The open question is whether societies that thrive on constant stimulation can rediscover silence not as absence but as presence, not as weakness but as strength. Can we learn, as earlier cultures did, to sit in stillness without fear, to treat quiet not as wasted time but as fertile ground? Or will silence remain, for us, the shock we would rather endure pain than face?

Why We Fear Stillness

In 2014, a widely reported study offered participants a peculiar choice: sit alone in silence for fifteen minutes or press a button that delivered an electric shock. A surprising number chose the shock. The finding seemed absurd—why would anyone prefer pain to peace? Yet it revealed something both ordinary and unsettling. For many, stillness is not rest but discomfort. Silence, rather than soothing, exposes a kind of rawness. It is as though, when external noise fades, the noise inside becomes unbearable.

This paradox runs deep. Ask people what they want from life, and peace is high on the list. Ask them to sit still for more than a few minutes, and they fidget, reach for their phones, or invent tasks. We crave calm, yet recoil from the conditions that make it possible. This tension is not trivial; it is a defining feature of modern restlessness. To understand why quiet feels so threatening, we must look at boredom, control, and the cultural suspicion of unoccupied time.

Psychologists studying boredom describe it not as an absence of stimulation but as a mismatch between what the mind demands and what the environment provides. In stillness, stripped of distraction, the restless brain goes looking for novelty and finds little. The result is agitation, a sense that time has slowed to a crawl. Evolutionarily, this made sense. Boredom pushed our ancestors to seek new opportunities, explore unfamiliar terrain, invent tools. But in today's world, where survival no longer requires constant novelty, the impulse lingers. Left alone in silence, the mind revolts, as if stillness were wasted time rather than fertile ground.

The modern economy exploits this unease. Entire industries depend on convincing us that idle minutes must be filled. Advertising tells us that boredom is failure; devices promise stimulation on demand. Even leisure is packaged as productivity—fitness tracked, reading logged, meditation gamified. In such a culture, stillness feels not only uncomfortable but irresponsible. To sit quietly is to step out of the current of optimisation, to risk appearing unproductive in a world that equates busyness with worth.

Loss of control is another source of resistance. In motion, in noise, we feel agency: we are doing something, shaping outcomes, pushing forward. Stillness removes that illusion. To be quiet is to confront the reality that much lies outside our control—uncertain futures, unresolved pasts, mortality itself. No wonder silence unsettles. It leaves us exposed to the very limits we try so hard to deny. The chatter of constant activity is not only distraction; it is armour against awareness of vulnerability.

This fear is evident across cultures. In the United States, conversational gaps are often rushed to be filled, as if silence signals incompetence or disconnection. In Japan, by contrast, silence can communicate respect, depth, or thoughtfulness. The discomfort is not universal, but it is deeply shaped by cultural assumptions about what it means to be present, valuable, alive. In societies where selfhood is defined by constant performance, stillness feels like absence. In societies where presence includes listening, stillness feels like fullness.

There is also a neurological dimension. The brain's default mode network, active when we are not focused externally, produces streams of self-referential thought. Left in silence, these thoughts grow louder. We replay mistakes, rehearse conversations, imagine threats. Stillness strips away distraction and leaves us with ourselves, unfiltered. For those unaccustomed to observing their own mind without judgement, the experience can feel like drowning. The fear of stillness, in this light, is less about silence itself and more about what silence reveals: the ceaseless voice within.

Yet paradoxically, it is only by enduring that discomfort that we can discover what lies beyond it. Monastic traditions across cultures understood this well. The Buddhist monk seated in meditation, the Christian nun in contemplative prayer, the Sufi in silent remembrance—all faced the turbulence of inner chatter before glimpsing clarity. They did not fear stillness but treated it as training, a crucible in which the mind's noise was not denied but observed until it softened. The traditions suggest that our fear of silence is not inevitable; it is a skill deficit. We have lost the capacity to sit quietly without fleeing.

Stillness threatens our habits of self-definition. In activity, we know who we are: the lawyer drafting briefs, the parent ferrying children, the student revising for exams. But in stillness, stripped of roles, what remains? For some, this absence is terrifying—a confrontation with identity beyond performance. For others, it can be liberating, a glimpse of selfhood not tethered to doing but to being. Which it becomes depends less on silence itself and more on how we meet it.

The deeper question is whether modern culture, so saturated with stimulation, can relearn the value of stillness. Can silence be reframed not as wasted time but as essential time? Can we train ourselves to sit with discomfort long enough to see that beneath boredom lies creativity, beneath agitation lies clarity, and beneath fear lies resilience? Or will we continue to choose the small shocks of distraction over the greater shock of facing ourselves?

Stillness is both what we long for and what we resist most. Whether we learn to embrace it may determine not only the quality of our attention but the depth of our lives.

Chapter 3
Meeting the Inner Narrator

Late at night, when the room falls silent and the world outside retreats, a different kind of voice often comes forward. It comments on the day's conversations, sometimes replaying them word for word. It second-guesses the choices made, forecasts the meetings to come, or mutters a quiet rebuke: *Why did you say that? You should have done better. You'll regret this tomorrow.* No one else can hear it, yet its presence is constant, weaving through thought like a soundtrack we cannot switch off.

This voice—the inner narrator—is not new. Writers have described it for centuries. The Stoics urged vigilance over it; Shakespeare gave Hamlet soliloquies that expose its ceaseless commentary; modern psychology has placed it at the centre of cognitive research. It is both interpreter and judge, capable of clarifying experience yet equally capable of distorting it. Some days, it offers perspective. Other days, it undermines confidence with a litany of doubts. The paradox is stark: the very voice that defines our inner life can also be the one that sabotages it.

To grasp its power, consider how the narrator shapes identity. The stories it tells us about who we are become the scaffolding of selfhood. A child who internalises the refrain *you're clumsy* may grow into an adult who hesitates before taking risks, long after the label has lost any basis in reality. A high-achieving professional who constantly hears *you're falling behind* may live in chronic restlessness, regardless of actual success. The narrator does not merely describe; it scripts. And when left unchecked, its script can confine us to roles we never consciously chose.

Cognitive behavioural therapy has illuminated how this voice tends to misfire. It catastrophises, insisting that one mistake at work will lead to dismissal. It engages in black-and-white thinking, framing outcomes as total success or utter failure. It personalises, interpreting ambiguous events as direct judgements: the friend who did not reply must secretly be angry. These distortions, once named, reveal the narrator's habits. They show that the inner voice is not infallible but patterned, prone to error, and capable of revision. Awareness is the first step in loosening its grip.

Yet to treat the narrator as an enemy to be silenced is a mistake. Without it, we lose the capacity to integrate memory, to imagine futures, to reflect on values. The voice that criticises us is also the one that helps us plan, that weighs options, that narrates the meaning of triumphs and losses alike. The challenge is not eradication but reorientation: to learn when the narrator is serving us and when it is leading us astray. To reframe it from saboteur to signal.

This chapter will move through these layers: first meeting the narrator as the constant presence it is, then examining the stories it spins, then naming the distortions that reveal its fallibility, and finally, exploring how it can be transformed into an ally. The payoff is more than intellectual. To master our relationship with this inner commentary is to shift from being its captive to being its author. The voice will always speak. The question is whether we remain subject to its script, or learn to write a new one.

What happens when we stop fighting the inner narrator and begin listening with discernment? What changes when the voice in our heads is no longer the loudest critic but the clearest guide? The path to that possibility begins with recognising that the narrator is not the enemy. It is us—and it can be rewritten.

The Voice in Your Head

On the morning of a crucial presentation, a young executive leaves home rehearsing her opening lines. As she walks, her mind races: *Don't stumble. Make eye contact. Don't let them see you're nervous.* Halfway through the rehearsal, another voice cuts in: *You're not ready. They'll see through you. You're going to fail.* She has not spoken aloud, yet her body responds—her stomach clenches, her heart rate rises, her palms sweat. Nothing external has happened. The voice in her head has shifted, and with it her entire experience of reality.

Everyone knows this voice. It narrates our lives with tireless persistence, commenting on the trivial and the profound alike. It praises us one moment, chastises us the next. It can function as coach, critic, analyst, or saboteur. Rarely does it rest. Some days it is background noise, barely noticed; other days it takes centre stage, dictating our mood, our confidence, even the decisions we dare to make. The question is not whether you have an inner narrator but how well you recognise its influence.

Psychologists sometimes describe this voice as a form of "inner speech," an ongoing commentary that shapes perception. It does more than observe events—it interprets them. Two people may encounter the same situation yet experience it entirely differently because their narrators spin contrasting stories. A driver cut off in traffic might hear: *He's reckless; I need to stay calm.* Another might hear: *He's disrespecting me; I can't let this go.* The external event is the same; the internal voice transforms it into a narrative of either irritation or rage.

Real-world vignettes reveal the narrator's subtle power. A student awaiting exam results might hear reassurance: *Whatever happens, I worked hard and will find a path forward.* Another, equally diligent, might hear only dread: *If I fail, everything is ruined.* In relationships, the voice interprets pauses, silences, tones of voice: *She doesn't care about me anymore* or *He's upset with me.* Sometimes the voice is accurate. More often, it overlays meaning that may or may not exist. Life, then, is lived not just in events but in the stories we tell about them.

Philosophers have long grappled with this inner commentary. Descartes's dictum *cogito, ergo sum*—"I think, therefore I am"—places thought at the core of existence. But lived experience suggests something sharper: *I narrate, therefore my world takes shape.* The voice inside us does not merely record; it organises reality into coherence, often at the cost of truth. It edits, distorts, dramatises, and occasionally consoles. It is not a passive witness but an active author, writing and rewriting the script of selfhood moment by moment.

Sometimes, the narrator brings clarity. Athletes describe hearing a focused inner voice in moments of peak performance: *Steady, breathe, trust your training.* Artists speak of guidance that helps them refine choices mid-creation: *This note is off, this brushstroke too harsh.* In such cases, the narrator sharpens awareness, offering feedback that aligns with skill and intention. Here, the voice is ally—an internal mentor enhancing rather than undermining.

But more often, it is the distortions that dominate. The catastrophising voice turns minor setbacks into imagined disasters: *One mistake means everything will collapse.* The perfectionist voice insists on impossible standards: *Unless it's flawless, it's worthless.* The anxious voice magnifies uncertainty: *If you don't plan for every possibility, you'll be blindsided.* These patterns are not arbitrary; they echo well-documented cognitive distortions. The voice becomes less like a fair observer and more like a prosecutor determined to secure conviction regardless of evidence.

What complicates matters is how seamlessly we identify with this inner voice. Most people do not pause to question it; they assume it *is* them. Yet when scrutinised, the voice often repeats scripts absorbed from parents, teachers, peers, or culture at large. The harsh critic may echo an early authority figure. The relentless perfectionist may embody societal ideals of productivity. The inner narrator, then, is not purely personal—it is an amalgam of influences, internalised until indistinguishable from self.

This insight can be liberating. If the narrator is not identical with self, it can be observed, questioned, even reshaped. A thought like *You're going to fail* can be met with: *That's just the anxious voice speaking again; it doesn't hold the whole truth.* With practice, the voice loses some of its tyranny. The narrator remains, but it is reframed as one perspective among many, not an oracle of absolute reality.

Still, the challenge persists. The voice in our head is tireless. Even in moments of apparent stillness, it speaks. Meditation practitioners often discover that when external silence deepens, the inner narrator grows louder, filling the gap. This is not a failure of practice but a revelation of how constant the voice truly is. To encounter it without judgement is to see clearly, perhaps for the first time, how much of life is mediated by internal commentary.

And so the central question emerges: can the voice become a companion rather than an adversary? Can it shift from distortion towards clarity, from critic towards guide? The narrator will not disappear. It will continue to spin stories, some helpful, some destructive. The task is to learn which stories to trust, which to challenge, and which to simply let pass. For if life is narrated from within, then learning to listen wisely may be the most essential skill of all.

The next step is not to silence the voice but to meet it—directly, honestly, without fear. Only then can we begin to decide which parts of its story are worth living by, and which are not. The voice in your head will keep speaking. The question is whether you will remain its captive, or become its editor.

Stories We Tell Ourselves

A young lawyer, outwardly accomplished, begins each morning with the same refrain in her head: *You're a fraud. Sooner or later, they'll find out.* The story is not spoken aloud, yet it governs her decisions—how she prepares for meetings, how she interprets the faintest criticism, how she minimises her successes. Objectively, she has evidence of competence. Subjectively, the story of inadequacy is louder.

This is the paradox at the core of the human mind: what matters most is not only what happens to us, but the narrative through which we interpret it.

We all live by such stories. They give coherence to the chaos of events, stitching them into patterns that define who we are. But these stories are not neutral; they are selective and interpretative. They highlight certain details while omitting others, casting us alternately as hero, victim, or villain in our own inner dramas. Some of these narratives help us grow, providing frameworks of meaning that sustain us in difficulty. Others distort reality, turning setbacks into evidence of permanent failure or translating ambition into relentless self-criticism.

Modern psychology recognises these narratives as central to identity. Narrative therapy, for instance, rests on the insight that the self is not a fixed essence but a story continually told and revised. The voice that says *I am unlucky in love* or *I never finish what I start* may feel like fact, but it is in truth a storyline constructed from selected memories and repeated often enough to harden into identity. To question the story is to loosen its hold; to retell it differently is to alter the self who lives inside it.

Yet our inner chatter rarely offers balanced storytelling. It tends towards extremes: exaggerating flaws, minimising strengths, predicting catastrophe. These tendencies echo cognitive distortions—patterns well documented in cognitive behavioural therapy. When the mind insists, *If I don't succeed perfectly, I'm worthless,* it is engaging in all-or-nothing thinking. When it interprets a colleague's distracted silence as rejection, it is personalisation. When it assumes that one rejection will lead to a lifetime of failure, it is catastrophising. Left unexamined, such distortions become the building blocks of a story that constrains rather than empowers.

Cultural forces amplify these patterns. In societies that idolise productivity, the inner story often takes the form of ceaseless self-criticism: *You are only as good as your latest achievement.* In cultures that prize external appearance, the narrative becomes one of perpetual inadequacy: *You will never measure up to the standard.* Social media intensifies both, offering curated feeds against which individuals measure their own messy realities. The story of self is no longer private but constantly compared, adjusted, and destabilised in relation to others.

There are, of course, counterexamples. Some individuals inherit or construct more generous inner narratives: *I am resilient; I can adapt.* These voices offer compassion rather than condemnation. They are not naïve; they acknowledge difficulty but frame it within a larger story of growth. The difference between these constructive stories and destructive ones is not that one is "true" and the other "false." Both are interpretations. The difference is which interpretation enables flourishing and which narrows the horizon of possibility.

Philosophers have long seen the dangers and power of self-narration. Nietzsche warned of the "tyranny of the little man within," the voice that belittles ambition and mocks striving. Buddhist thinkers described the self as a bundle of stories mistaken for essence, encouraging practices that reveal their impermanence. In a different register, modern neuroscientists studying the default mode network find that when the brain is at rest, it generates precisely this sort of autobiographical chatter. Left unchecked, the mind defaults to self-storying, endlessly rehearsing the past and projecting futures, often with a negative bias.

Yet if our identities are indeed storied, then the possibility exists to edit, to re-author. This is not the simplistic advice of "positive affirmations," which often ring hollow. It is a subtler act: noticing the story being told, testing its assumptions against reality, and considering alternative plotlines. The lawyer who repeats *I'm a fraud* might counter with evidence: years of successful cases, recognition from peers, the objective fact that mistakes are part of growth. Over time, the counter-story—*I am competent and learning*—may gain strength, reshaping both experience and identity.

The difficulty lies in how deeply we are fused with our stories. They feel like us. To question them can feel like questioning the self itself. But the truth is more liberating: the self is not a single story but a library of possible tellings. The voice that insists you are inadequate is not the only narrator available. The challenge is learning to discern when a story is guiding wisely and when it is imprisoning, when it clarifies reality and when it distorts it.

This raises a provocative possibility: what if the stories we tell ourselves are less about uncovering who we "truly" are and more about deciding who we are becoming? What if identity is not a fixed narrative but an ongoing draft? If so, the voice in your head is not merely reporting on you—it is shaping you. Whether it shapes with cruelty or compassion, with rigidity or flexibility, depends on how consciously you engage with it.

The stories we tell ourselves can crush us under their weight, or they can steady us as we move forward. The question that remains is whether we will continue to live by inherited scripts or begin to write ones that allow us to live with clarity, resilience, and depth.

Spotting Cognitive Distortions

In 1979, psychologist Aaron Beck asked a patient to describe why she believed she was worthless. Her answer was swift: *Because I made a mistake yesterday, and people must think I'm incompetent.* To Beck, it was a striking example of what he called "cognitive distortions"—patterns of thought that bend reality into rigid, self-defeating shapes. What the patient saw as evidence of worthlessness was, in truth, a common human error reframed as a global judgement. That single encounter helped crystallise one of the most powerful insights in modern psychology: the way we *think about thinking* matters as much as what happens to us.

Cognitive distortions are not exotic flaws reserved for the mentally ill. They are the ordinary errors of a mind evolved for survival, not for accuracy. The inner narrator does not simply record reality; it edits, dramatises, and often exaggerates. To recognise these distortions is not to expose weakness but to gain literacy in the architecture of thought. For the stories we live by are written in their patterns, and until those patterns are named, they remain invisible.

Consider catastrophising, perhaps the most dramatic of these distortions. A missed call from a supervisor becomes, in the mind's theatre, the first act of dismissal. A partner's sigh at the dinner table becomes the prelude to abandonment. The leap from event to apocalypse is swift and convincing. Evolution favoured this habit: better to overestimate danger than underestimate it. But in the modern world, where sabre-toothed tigers are rare, catastrophising corrodes daily life. It keeps the nervous system in a perpetual state of alarm, as though every shadow conceals disaster.

Equally insidious is black-and-white thinking. Here, nuance is banished in favour of absolutes: success or failure, love or rejection, perfect or worthless. A student earning 85% interprets it not as achievement but as failure because it is not 100. A parent missing one school event condemns themselves as inadequate. Life, however, rarely conforms to absolutes. It unfolds in gradients. Yet the narrator, addicted to simplicity, prefers the blunt clarity of extremes, even when it misrepresents reality.

Personalisation, too, distorts. It interprets ambiguous events as self-referential. The colleague who fails to smile must be harbouring resentment. The traffic jam is not mere congestion but a personal assault on one's time. Children, especially, are prone to this. A child of divorcing parents may quietly decide: *This is my fault.* The mind inserts itself into every drama, even when the evidence is thin. The distortion is not arrogance but a by-product of our social wiring; we are primed to see ourselves as central to the narrative, lest we miss cues that once governed survival in tight-knit groups.

What unites these distortions is their plausibility. They arrive in the voice of inner authority, sounding less like errors than truths. Rarely do they declare themselves as distortions. Instead, they masquerade as reason: *Of course this will end badly. Of course they are disappointed in me. Of course I'm to blame.* This makes them difficult to detect from the inside. To spot them requires both education and distance—a willingness to step back and treat the narrator not as oracle but as suspect witness.

Real-world cases illuminate the cost. A surgeon, haunted by one complication in an otherwise successful career, begins to hear the inner voice say, *You are dangerous; you should stop operating.* Catastrophising merges with personalisation, threatening a vocation. A teenager, receiving no reply to a message, constructs a narrative of rejection: *They hate me. I have no friends.* Black-and-white thinking tightens the loop, fuelling isolation. In both examples, the distortion is not trivial—it shapes decisions, relationships, and identity itself.

The counterpoint, however, is hopeful: distortions lose power once named. The lawyer who recognises the leap from missed call to imagined dismissal can pause and ask, *What evidence do I have?* The parent who hears the voice of inadequacy can reframe, *Missing one event does not erase years of care.* Naming a distortion is like turning on a light in a dark room; the shadows remain, but they are less convincing. Cognitive behavioural therapy is built on this insight, showing that the act of identifying and challenging distortions is itself corrective.

Philosophically, the practice has deeper resonance. To name a distortion is to admit that perception is not identical with reality, that the inner narrator is fallible. This humility opens space for flexibility. It shifts the stance from *I am my thoughts* to *I have thoughts, and some are inaccurate.* In that shift lies freedom—the freedom to resist being wholly defined by mental chatter, to respond with choice rather than compulsion.

Yet a lingering tension remains. If distortions are universal, can they ever be eliminated? Or is the task not eradication but management, learning to live with a mind that will always lean towards exaggeration? Perhaps the measure of mental clarity is not the absence of distortions but the speed with which we catch them, the grace with which we correct them, and the gentleness with which we forgive ourselves for having them at all.

The narrator will continue to tell its stories. Some will be helpful, others warped. The crucial question is whether we can learn to recognise its distortions not as immutable truths but as habits of thought—habits that can be interrupted, questioned, and reshaped. For only by spotting the distortions can we hope to rewrite the story they create.

From Enemy to Ally

One of the most striking ironies of the human mind is that the voice we most often wish to silence may also be the one most capable of guiding us. The inner narrator—so frequently accused of sabotage with its criticisms, doubts, and rehearsals of catastrophe—does not exist to torment. It exists to protect. It evolved as a survival mechanism, anticipating danger, rehearsing responses, and making sense of experience. The trouble is not its presence but our relationship with it. To treat it solely as an enemy is to miss the possibility of transformation.

Take the story of an elite athlete preparing for competition. Her narrator whispers: *You'll choke, you're not ready.* Initially, this voice undermines, threatening paralysis. Yet with training, she learns to reinterpret it—not as prophecy but as signal. The voice of doubt becomes evidence of high stakes, a reminder to focus, to draw on practice, to steady the breath. The words remain, but their meaning shifts. What once felt like sabotage becomes fuel. This shift—from enemy to ally—is not about silencing the narrator but about hearing it differently.

Psychologists have long noted this distinction. Suppression, the attempt to banish unwanted thoughts, rarely succeeds. Studies show that trying not to think about something—whether a craving, a fear, or even the classic "white bear"—only makes it more persistent. The same holds for the inner critic. The more we try to mute it, the louder it becomes. Mastery lies elsewhere: in reframing. By recognising the narrator as a part of ourselves, we can choose how to respond to it rather than be compelled by it.

Consider how this reframing works in everyday contexts. A student hearing *You're going to fail this exam* can treat it as sabotage, spiralling into panic. Or she can treat it as signal: the voice points to anxiety, which in turn signals the importance of rest, preparation, or perspective. A professional haunted by *You're falling behind* may either collapse under its weight or notice that the voice is highlighting areas where he feels disconnected from his values. The same sentence, interpreted differently, shifts from obstacle to guide.

This does not mean the narrator is always right. Like a well-meaning but anxious parent, it often overstates danger, underestimates capacity, or clings to outdated scripts. But even its distortions can be instructive. Catastrophising reveals where we feel most vulnerable. Black-and-white thinking exposes rigid standards. Personalisation shows our longing for connection. In each case, the voice carries information—not accurate about reality, but accurate about our inner terrain. To hear it in this way is to treat it less as saboteur and more as messenger.

Philosophically, this reframing echoes ancient traditions. The Stoics did not aim to erase emotion but to reinterpret it, treating fear and anger as signals to examine assumptions. Buddhist practice regards thoughts not as enemies but as clouds passing across awareness—neither to be grasped nor denied, but observed and understood. Modern psychology, too, aligns with this view: cognitive defusion techniques from Acceptance and Commitment Therapy teach individuals to step back from thoughts, seeing them as words and sounds rather than absolute truths. The wisdom converges: mastery lies not in suppression but in altered relationship.

The implications for identity are profound. If the narrator is not enemy, then selfhood need not be a battlefield. Instead of fighting our thoughts, we can learn to collaborate with them, to listen for what they reveal about fear, desire, and values. The critic who insists, *You're not good enough,* may be pointing to a deeper yearning for growth or for recognition. The anxious planner who spins endless "what-ifs" may be expressing a desire for safety. Beneath the surface noise lies a signal worth hearing.

This reframing is not easy. It requires practice, patience, and a willingness to sit with discomfort rather than flee from it. But the reward is significant: a quieter mind not because the narrator has been silenced but because its voice has been integrated, its messages sifted, its distortions softened. Over time, the narrator becomes less like a hostile force and more like a companion whose quirks are understood and managed.

The question, then, is not whether the inner narrator will speak—it always will—but how we will listen. Will we hear its criticisms as verdicts, or as signals to examine? Will we treat its fears as commands, or as reminders of what matters? Can we learn to meet the voice with curiosity rather than hostility, discernment rather than submission?

If we can, then the inner narrator ceases to be a saboteur and becomes an ally—sometimes clumsy, sometimes harsh, but ultimately a source of information that can deepen awareness and sharpen resilience. The voice in your head will always be there. The choice is whether you continue to fight it, or whether you begin to hear, beneath its noise, the signal it has been offering all along.

Chapter 4
The Science of Thought Loops

On a crowded commuter train, a man sits staring at nothing in particular. To those around him, he looks absent. Yet inside his mind, whole worlds unfold. He replays a conversation from yesterday, adjusting his words in an endless loop. He leaps forward to tomorrow's meeting, rehearsing possible outcomes. He drifts sideways to a fantasy of escape, picturing himself in a quiet house by the sea. Outwardly still, inwardly in motion, his mind churns through a private theatre of past, future, and imagined scenes. He is not alone. This mental wandering is one of the most universal features of human consciousness—and one of the most poorly understood.

The paradox is striking. When the body rests, the brain becomes more active. Even in moments of quiet—waiting in a queue, drifting before sleep, pausing between tasks—the mind rarely idles. Neuroscientists call this pattern the *default mode network,* the circuitry that lights up when attention is not anchored on the outside world. It is here, in this backstage of thought, that loops form: the constant rehearsals, replays, and predictions that define inner chatter. What feels like distraction is, in fact, the brain's baseline state.

To understand thought loops is to confront a fundamental truth about the brain: it is a prediction machine. Evolution shaped it not to dwell serenely in the present but to anticipate. It scans backwards to extract lessons from the past, then projects forwards to simulate outcomes. This cycle once kept our ancestors alive, helping them recall which berries poisoned and which shelters protected, while imagining dangers that might lie ahead. But in the modern world, the same circuitry can become a trap. The "what ifs" multiply beyond usefulness, spiralling into rumination and anxiety. The very gift of foresight becomes the burden of incessant noise.

Stress intensifies this cycle. When cortisol floods the system, the predictive machinery speeds up, generating an avalanche of scenarios, each more urgent than the last. What began as a mechanism for survival turns into chronic static: an executive unable to sleep before a deadline, a parent catastrophising every small cough in their child, a student paralysed by imagined futures. Stress does not only weigh on the body; it amplifies the mind's loops until they drown out clarity.

This raises a critical question: if looping is the brain's default, is there any escape? The answer lies in attention. Unlike the automatic drift of thought, attention is a scarce and deliberate resource. To train attention is to create a counterweight to the loops—to choose where the mind lingers rather than be carried by its momentum. Yet attention is fragile. In a world engineered for distraction, it fragments easily, leaving the loops to reclaim control.

The stakes are both personal and collective. On the individual level, unchecked loops sap energy, erode decision-making, and cloud identity. On the societal level, they scale up into cultures of burnout, polarisation, and constant crisis—worlds where attention is perpetually hijacked, and clarity is rare. To study the science of thought loops is not an academic exercise; it is an inquiry into how we live, how we suffer, and how we might reclaim steadiness in a time of overload.

This chapter examines the loops not as curiosities but as central features of mind. We will explore the default mode network and its restless theatre of thought; the predictive coding that drives us to replay and rehearse; the biological impact of stress that floods cognition with noise; and the fragile, vital role of attention as the lever through which loops can be interrupted. Together, these strands reveal why our minds so easily spiral—and how understanding the mechanics of looping opens the door to quieting it.

The loops will not vanish. But they need not dictate. By tracing their science, we gain the first glimpse of mastery: the ability to see thought for what it is—pattern, habit, circuitry—rather than destiny. The next step is learning how to work with these loops rather than be consumed by them, a step that begins here.

The Default Mode Network

In 1997, a young neuroscientist named Marcus Raichle noticed something curious. During brain scans, even when subjects were asked to do nothing—no tasks, no puzzles, no sensory input—their brains lit up with activity. Far from idling, the brain seemed to switch into another mode altogether. This "background hum" was not noise; it was patterned, organised, and astonishingly consistent across individuals. What Raichle and his colleagues stumbled upon became one of the most influential discoveries in modern neuroscience: the *default mode network*.

The paradox is arresting. The moments when we appear most still—daydreaming on a train, brushing our teeth, staring out of a window—are often when the brain is most active. In fact, the brain consumes nearly as much energy at rest as it does when engaged in demanding tasks. This default state is not passive; it is a theatre of spontaneous thought. Here, we wander through memories, imagine future scenarios, rehearse conversations, and drift into fantasies. The *default* is not silence but a chorus of voices: past, present, and possible selves colliding in mental rehearsal.

At its core, the default mode network (DMN) links regions of the brain concerned with memory, self-reflection, and imagination: the medial prefrontal cortex, posterior cingulate cortex, and angular gyrus, among others. When these areas synchronise, they generate the experience of an inner narrator weaving fragments into stories. Neuroscientists sometimes describe the DMN as the seat of "autobiographical thinking," the system that allows us to place ourselves in time—who we were, who we are, who we might become.

This function is adaptive. By replaying the past, the brain extracts lessons: the predator hid in that clearing; the colleague responded badly to that phrasing; the investment failed for that reason. By simulating the future, it generates foresight: *If I say this, what might happen? If I take that road, what could go wrong?* In evolutionary terms, this constant rehearsal was priceless. Anticipation conferred survival. The DMN made us not only Homo sapiens—knowing humans—but *Homo prospectus*: humans who imagine what is next.

Yet the same machinery that equips us for foresight also entangles us in loops. The DMN does not discriminate between useful rehearsal and futile rumination. It can as easily replay humiliation from years ago as it can refine tomorrow's presentation. It can dwell on mistakes with no resolution, or conjure catastrophes that never occur. In this way, the gift of a self-narrating brain becomes the burden of incessant chatter.

Modern life magnifies this burden. The DMN is hypersensitive to stress. Elevated cortisol pushes the network into overdrive, flooding consciousness with intrusive thoughts. Anxieties replay endlessly, as though the brain believes that more rehearsal will somehow resolve uncertainty. In truth, the opposite happens: the circuitry entrenches itself, wiring ruts of worry and regret. Neuroscientists observing overactive DMNs in functional MRI scans see striking correlations with depression, anxiety, and even creativity gone awry. The very network that allows Shakespeare to imagine Hamlet's soliloquies also traps an insomniac in a midnight loop of "what ifs."

At the same time, the DMN is not inherently pathological. It is also the source of some of our richest capacities. It fuels imagination, allowing artists to conceive new worlds, scientists to model hypotheses, and children to invent games from sticks and shadows. Daydreaming, long maligned as idle distraction, has been reframed as essential incubation for insight. Many breakthroughs in science and art have emerged not during focused labour but while the DMN was roaming—Einstein envisioning himself riding a beam of light, or Kekulé dreaming of a snake biting its tail and discovering the structure of benzene.

The philosophical implications are striking. The DMN suggests that the "self" is less a stable entity than an ongoing construction, continually authored in the brain's resting state. Our identities emerge not only from external events but from the constant rehearsal of those events in imagination. In this sense, the DMN is both the architect and the echo chamber of selfhood. It preserves continuity but also amplifies distortion. When unchecked, it convinces us that the story it spins—of failure, rejection, inadequacy—is reality itself.

What, then, are we to do with this restless network? Suppression is impossible; the DMN is wired into the architecture of mind. But awareness changes the relationship. Mindfulness practices, for example, do not deactivate the DMN entirely but shift its patterns. Meditators show reduced activity in regions tied to self-referential rumination and increased connectivity with areas that regulate attention. This suggests that the DMN can be trained—not silenced, but guided.

The unresolved tension is this: the DMN is both curse and gift. It enslaves us in loops of worry, yet enables the foresight and imagination that define humanity. It generates suffering when left untended, yet creativity when gently harnessed. To understand it is to confront a paradox at the heart of consciousness: that the brain's resting state is not rest at all, but ceaseless storytelling. The challenge is not to escape this network but to learn how to live with it, to use its wanderings as signal rather than static.

If the DMN is our default, the pressing question becomes: how do we learn to step out of default and into choice? How do we reclaim authority over a system designed to run in the background? The answers are neither simple nor final—but they begin with recognising that the voice in your head is not noise alone. It is the architecture of imagination itself, waiting to be shaped.

Why We Replay and Predict

A woman lies awake at three in the morning, eyes fixed on the ceiling. She replays a conversation with her manager, dissecting every phrase, every shift of tone, searching for the moment where it went wrong. No sooner has she exhausted the past than her mind launches forward into the future: *What if this ruins my prospects? What if I can't recover? What if I never sleep again?* By dawn she is exhausted, not from labour but from the endless work of anticipation. Her plight is painfully common. The human mind, uniquely gifted with foresight, cannot resist the compulsion to replay and predict.

The paradox is ancient: the very capacity that makes us intelligent—our ability to remember and to imagine—also binds us in chains of *what if.* Unlike other animals, we can rehearse conversations before they occur, envision outcomes never yet experienced, and learn vicariously from remembered mistakes. This talent for simulation allowed us to become architects, strategists, storytellers. Yet it also explains why so many of us find ourselves caught in loops of regret and anxiety. Our brains are prediction engines, and prediction never stops running.

Neuroscience provides a clue as to why. The brain does not merely receive information about the world; it constantly generates models of what it expects to encounter. This process, known as *predictive coding,* suggests that perception itself is not passive but an active guess, a forecast of incoming reality. We are always living partly in the future. The crack of a twig makes us anticipate a predator before we confirm it is only the wind. A colleague's expression primes us to interpret annoyance before a word is spoken. This machinery of anticipation is indispensable—but it is also the source of endless chatter.

Replaying the past serves prediction too. The mind re-enacts arguments, missed opportunities, or social encounters not for nostalgia's sake but as training material. By re-running the past, the brain adjusts its models of the future. Yet in modern contexts—where threats are rarely tigers in the grass but emails in the inbox—the same rehearsal can spiral without resolution. Unlike concrete dangers, many of today's triggers remain open-ended. The argument can be re-lived a hundred times without yielding a single lesson. The prediction machine spins, but no clarity emerges.

Real-world examples illustrate this vividly. Athletes visualise races again and again, a constructive form of replay that sharpens performance. But a traumatised soldier relives combat scenes involuntarily, caught in the brain's desperate attempt to anticipate danger. A professional might rehearse a presentation until it flows with confidence, while another obsesses over a single mistake in last week's meeting, unable to move forward. The same predictive system is at work in each case. Its outputs differ not in mechanism but in how they are harnessed—or hijacked.

Philosophically, this invites reflection on the cost of imagination. The Stoics warned against "suffering more in imagination than in reality," recognising the mind's tendency to magnify possibilities into certainties. Eastern contemplative traditions similarly counselled anchoring in the present, observing how the mind leaps forward or back in ceaseless commentary. Both perspectives converge with modern science: our torment lies less in what happens than in the endless replay of what has happened and anticipation of what might.

One striking feature of predictive loops is their resistance to closure. Unlike physical tasks, mental simulations rarely finish. A carpenter sands until the wood is smooth; a runner stops at the finish line. But a mind rehearsing "what if I fail" finds no endpoint, because the future remains perpetually open. This lack of closure is exhausting. The brain craves resolution, yet prediction keeps it suspended, tugging attention back to scenarios it cannot settle. The result is a restless inner theatre that feels urgent but rarely useful.

There is also a cultural dimension. Societies that valorise planning and productivity intensify these loops. The pressure to anticipate every outcome, to stay ahead, to optimise every choice, rewards the predictive brain even as it drives individuals towards burnout. Technology magnifies this further: constant notifications and rolling news cycles feed the sense that something is always about to happen, demanding our foresight. In such conditions, prediction ceases to be a tool and becomes a compulsion.

Yet we cannot—and should not—switch it off. The predictive mind is the source of creativity, strategy, and resilience. It allows scientists to hypothesise, doctors to anticipate complications, parents to safeguard children. The challenge lies in discerning when prediction serves and when it enslaves. When does a rehearsal sharpen our ability, and when does it collapse into paralysis? When does remembering a failure prepare us, and when does it merely reopen wounds?

The unresolved tension is this: we need the predictive brain to live wisely, but we also need to guard against its overreach. The loops will not disappear; they are woven into the fabric of thought. The task is to notice when they are running unchecked, to ask whether replay or projection is yielding clarity or only static. Can we learn to inhabit the present without abandoning foresight? Can the same machinery that traps us in "what if" also guide us towards "what matters"?

The mind will replay and predict regardless. The question, left hanging, is whether we continue to follow it blindly—or whether we can learn to step back, watch the loops spin, and decide when to listen.

Stress, Cortisol, and Mental Static

Imagine a worker stepping into the office each morning already weary from a night of fractured sleep. The body feels tense, the chest tight, the mind preoccupied with a mental checklist that never quite shrinks. Emails arrive faster than they can be answered, interruptions fracture attention, and by mid-afternoon even simple decisions feel like heavy burdens. Nothing catastrophic has happened; yet the nervous system hums as though danger lurks. This is the lived experience of chronic stress—not a single overwhelming event, but an unrelenting accumulation of demands that keeps the body's alarm bells ringing long after the fire should have been put out.

The paradox is clear. Stress, in short bursts, sharpens us. It primes us to act, focuses attention, mobilises energy. A surge of cortisol—the body's main stress hormone—was once a life-saving adaptation, helping our ancestors flee predators or endure famine. Yet in today's world, that same hormonal system is activated not by lions but by spreadsheets, deadlines, traffic jams, and a ceaseless stream of digital alerts. The ancient mechanism cannot distinguish between an existential threat and an inconvenient email. What once protected us now overwhelms us.

Cortisol is at the centre of this story. Secreted by the adrenal glands under the control of the hypothalamic–pituitary–adrenal (HPA) axis, it orchestrates the body's stress response. In acute episodes, cortisol boosts glucose availability, raises blood pressure, and sharpens awareness—physiology aligning with survival. But when stress becomes chronic, cortisol lingers in the bloodstream, dysregulating the very systems it was designed to protect. Memory falters, the immune system weakens, and the brain's networks of attention and self-regulation become hijacked by noise.

The effects on cognition are particularly striking. Prolonged cortisol exposure disrupts the hippocampus, a brain region crucial for memory, and the prefrontal cortex, which governs attention and executive control. Meanwhile, it strengthens circuits in the amygdala, heightening sensitivity to perceived threats. The result is a brain skewed towards vigilance and worry. Thoughts race, scenarios loop, risks are exaggerated. What began as a mechanism for clarity devolves into mental static—a kind of cognitive interference where nothing settles into coherence.

Real-world examples illustrate how insidious this process can be. Consider the phenomenon of "decision fatigue," where individuals facing constant micro-choices—from selecting meals to managing digital notifications—become progressively less capable of sound judgment. Studies show that judges are more likely to deny parole later in the day, when their cognitive reserves have been depleted. Physicians under high stress demonstrate increased error rates. Entrepreneurs under chronic pressure report difficulty distinguishing urgent problems from trivial ones. Each case reflects the same biology: cortisol narrowing attention, amplifying perceived risks, and cluttering the mind with intrusive thought.

Chronic stress also leaves its mark on relationships. When the nervous system is perpetually on alert, irritability and defensiveness rise. Communication breaks down; empathy diminishes. Partners interpret neutral remarks as criticism, colleagues misread intention, friends retreat rather than engage. In this sense; cortisol is not only a hormone of survival but also of social distortion. It narrows the bandwidth through which we interpret others, heightening conflict while eroding connection.

Philosophically, the consequences run deeper. The human mind evolved to anticipate danger and secure safety. But when the predictive brain is flooded with cortisol, it becomes trapped in a kind of false urgency, projecting threats into every corner of experience. The future feels hostile even when no danger exists. The result is not simply stress but an altered relationship to time itself: a life lived perpetually on the edge of an imagined crisis.

Modern culture compounds the effect. The ethic of constant productivity, the valorisation of busyness, the glamourisation of the "hustle" normalise stress as a badge of honour. To admit exhaustion is framed as weakness; to disconnect is to risk falling behind. Yet the biology tells a different story. A system wired for short bursts of stress collapses under the weight of continuous activation. The consequence is burnout, an epidemic condition defined not only by fatigue but by cynicism, disconnection, and a hollowing out of purpose.

And yet, the stress response cannot be dismissed as wholly destructive. It remains a vital part of human adaptability. The challenge is not to eradicate cortisol but to restore its rhythm. Cortisol is meant to peak in the morning, fuelling alertness, and decline in the evening, allowing rest. Under chronic stress, that rhythm flattens, leaving the body simultaneously wired and depleted. Understanding this cycle reframes the task: not silencing stress, but regulating it—allowing activation when needed, quiet when possible.

The unresolved question lingers: how do we live in a world where demands are continuous, yet our biology is tuned for pauses? How do we reclaim mental clarity in a culture that mistakes exhaustion for virtue? These questions cannot be answered by biology alone. They demand cultural rethinking, personal practice, and a willingness to challenge the noise both outside and within. Until then, many of us will remain like the worker staring at the ceiling at three a.m.—alert, exhausted, and trapped in the static of a system that never switches off.

The Role of Attention

A monk in a Zen monastery once remarked that enlightenment is nothing mystical—it is simply "attention, uninterrupted." The simplicity of the statement conceals a profound truth: attention is the fundamental currency of consciousness, the resource upon which all perception, memory, and decision-making depend. Yet in our daily lives it is the one resource we squander most carelessly. We guard our money, ration our time, even track our steps, but our attention is pulled haphazardly from screen to screen, notification to notification, leaving us scattered and restless.

The paradox is this: the human brain processes more sensory data every second than it could ever consciously absorb, and yet we experience only what we attend to. A pianist hears her mistakes not because the wrong notes are louder, but because her attention is primed to catch them. A driver on a motorway might suddenly notice every red car after deciding to buy one. Attention selects, filters, and shapes the reality we inhabit. It is at once powerful and perilously limited.

Neuroscience has made this limitation starkly clear. Experiments on "attentional bottlenecks" reveal that the brain can only hold a few items in working memory at once—perhaps four, at best. When demands exceed this capacity, the system falters. Cognitive psychologists speak of "switching costs": every time attention flips from one task to another, milliseconds are lost, errors creep in, and the mind fatigues. The much-celebrated myth of multitasking is in fact the slow erosion of focus, dressed up as efficiency.

The consequences go beyond productivity. Attention is the very mechanism by which mental noise either grows or recedes. Chatter feeds on untrained attention, pulling it compulsively toward what-if scenarios, regrets, or imagined criticisms. The more attention flits, the more it amplifies static. Conversely, attention trained to rest, to focus deliberately, can quieten the loops of inner narration. In this sense, attention is not merely a mental faculty but the gateway to clarity.

Consider real-world examples. An elite archer steadies her breath, narrowing attention to the target, and in that moment the crowd disappears. A surgeon in the operating theatre experiences "flow," where all distractions fall away and every ounce of attention fuses with the task. These are not mystical states but demonstrations of a disciplined resource at work. Compare them to the scattered professional who tries to draft a report while fielding emails, text messages, and news alerts. Each demand pulls at limited capacity, leaving the mind frayed, decisions rushed, and errors multiplied. The contrast could not be sharper.

Philosophy, too, has long recognised this dynamic. William James, often called the father of modern psychology, declared that "the faculty of voluntarily bringing back a wandering attention over and over again is the very root of judgment, character, and will." Centuries earlier, Buddhist traditions spoke of *sati*—mindfulness—as the cultivation of steady attention. Both point to the same truth: mastery of attention is mastery of the self. Without it, we are at the mercy of passing thoughts and external stimuli. With it, we can choose what matters.

Attention is also bound up with emotion. Under stress, cortisol skews attention towards threat, narrowing perspective to potential danger. This can save a life in an emergency, but in everyday contexts it fuels anxiety and hyper-vigilance. The mind becomes a searchlight fixed on risk, unable to widen its beam. Conversely, states of calm broaden attention, allowing creativity and empathy to emerge. This interplay helps explain why training attention is not only a cognitive skill but an emotional practice: where attention goes, mood follows.

Modern technology has made the stakes even higher. Platforms designed to monetise attention exploit its vulnerabilities. Infinite scrolling, push notifications, personalised feeds—all bypass deliberate choice, hooking the mind into compulsive loops. What began as tools of communication have become engines of distraction, draining attention with ruthless efficiency. In this context, training attention is not just a personal practice but a form of resistance, a reclamation of sovereignty over one's mental life.

Yet attention cannot be endlessly tightened like a muscle. It requires rhythms of focus and release, effort and rest. The great composers knew this: silence between notes gives music its shape. Likewise, the deliberate redirection of attention towards stillness—the breath, the body, the present moment—prepares the mind to meet the world with steadiness rather than static. Training attention is less about constant vigilance than about learning when to narrow, when to broaden, and when to let go altogether.

The open question is whether, in a world built to scatter us, we can restore attention to its rightful place. Can we treat it not as an expendable commodity but as the essence of our freedom? Can we learn, individually and collectively, to train attention so that the mind no longer serves every flicker of noise, but listens deliberately to what matters? The answer, perhaps, will determine not only the quietness of our minds but the quality of our lives.

Chapter 5
Learning to Watch Your Mind

Imagine sitting in a crowded theatre, the curtain rising to reveal not actors on a stage but the constant stream of your own thoughts. Some are familiar characters—anxious predictions, half-remembered conversations, unresolved lists—while others appear suddenly, without invitation, only to vanish as quickly as they arrived. For most of us, life passes in this theatre without ever realising that we are not the script, nor the actors, nor even the plot, but the audience itself. To watch the performance rather than be swept away by it is the essence of metacognition: the ability to think about thinking, to take a step back and witness the workings of the mind.

This idea is not new, though modern psychology has given it fresh language. Ancient contemplative traditions urged seekers to find the "witness within," a vantage point from which they could observe their thoughts as passing phenomena rather than absolute truths. Cognitive science, centuries later, reached a similar conclusion: that awareness of thought processes enables self-regulation, emotional balance, and deliberate choice. What once sounded mystical now emerges as an evidence-based cornerstone of mental clarity.

To watch one's mind is to reclaim distance. Without this distance, thoughts arrive like commands: a worry declares catastrophe; a memory insists on guilt; an idea demands immediate pursuit. But with awareness, a subtle gap opens. The thought becomes visible as just that—a thought, not a fact. In that pause lies possibility: to engage or let go, to act or remain still, to interpret or simply notice. This chapter is about that pause, and the discipline of making it wide enough to transform one's relationship with the inner narrator.

The significance of this shift cannot be overstated. Most of the world's mental noise is not harmful because the thoughts themselves are dangerous, but because we mistake them for reality. A flash of self-criticism—"I always fail at this"—becomes an unquestioned identity. A hypothetical worry—"What if the worst happens?"—spins into a full-body stress response. When awareness is absent, chatter masquerades as truth. When awareness is present, chatter reveals itself as chatter, and something remarkable happens: we are no longer trapped inside the monologue.

Throughout this chapter we will explore what it means to cultivate such awareness. We begin with metacognition defined—not as an abstract academic concept, but as a practical, lived skill that underpins every form of self-mastery. From there, we move to the metaphorical "observer's seat," techniques drawn from both mindfulness and neuroscience that teach us how to occupy this vantage point. We will examine *cognitive defusion*, a practice central to Acceptance and Commitment Therapy, which helps loosen the grip of thought by separating the thinker from the thought. And finally, we will explore how this progression leads to freedom: the shift from compulsive reaction to deliberate choice.

The invitation is both radical and deeply human. To watch your mind is to question its authority without disowning it, to acknowledge the ceaseless chatter while learning not to obey its every command. If attention is the gateway to clarity, then metacognition is the architecture that allows clarity to hold. The question before us is whether we can live as spectators and participants at once—able to step back, able to step in, never fully captive to either role. That tension is where the power lies, and it is where we now turn.

Metacognition Defined

Picture the moment just before you speak in a difficult meeting. Words queue in your mind, each one competing to be chosen, and yet—before any sound leaves your lips—you hesitate. You hear yourself thinking about what you might say, weighing its consequences, rehearsing its delivery. In that pause lies a peculiar kind of awareness: not the thought itself, but the awareness of having the thought. This is metacognition, the mind's ability to watch itself at work. It is at once utterly ordinary and profoundly mysterious.

The paradox of metacognition is that it is invisible until you notice it. A fish does not see the water until it leaps into the air; in the same way, most of us swim through streams of thought without recognising that we can step back and watch them flow. The moment you do, however, the texture of inner life changes. A worry becomes not an unquestioned certainty but a mental event you can observe, name, and even redirect. This ability—thinking about thinking—forms the foundation of self-awareness and, by extension, of freedom.

Psychologists began formally naming this phenomenon in the 1970s, but in truth, its recognition is far older. Philosophers from Socrates to Descartes, spiritual traditions from Buddhism to Sufism, all in their own ways pointed toward the mind's capacity to notice itself. What modern science added was the precision to test and measure it: metacognition allows us to assess our own learning, to detect errors before they solidify, and to recalibrate when reality contradicts expectation. It is the inner feedback loop that keeps us aligned with truth rather than illusion.

Consider a simple example: you are reading a dense article and suddenly realise you have absorbed nothing from the past three paragraphs. The recognition itself—"I wasn't paying attention"—is a metacognitive act. It allows you to stop, reread, and adjust your focus. Without that recognition, you would drift on, believing you were learning when you were not. Multiply this across the domains of decision-making, relationships, and moral judgment, and the stakes become clear: the ability to observe the quality of your own thinking determines whether you act with clarity or stumble blindly into error.

But metacognition is not always comfortable. To think about your thinking is also to confront its biases, its fragility, its compulsions. A lawyer preparing a case might recognise that her conviction is coloured more by personal emotion than by evidence. A student, confident in a quick answer, might catch the flicker of doubt and realise he has overlooked a crucial detail. These moments of discomfort are gifts; they reveal the boundary between illusion and accuracy, between assumption and understanding. Without them, the mind remains at the mercy of its first impulses.

This self-reflective stance becomes particularly important when we encounter the mental chatter that fills our days. The narrator in our head speaks with authority, weaving stories about who we are and what the world expects of us. Left unchecked, it is easy to confuse its voice with truth. Metacognition, however, offers distance: the ability to ask, *Is this thought accurate? Helpful? Necessary?* By interrogating the commentary rather than being absorbed by it, we loosen its grip and regain the possibility of choice.

Educational research has shown that students who practise metacognitive strategies—such as planning how to approach a problem, monitoring comprehension, and evaluating progress—outperform those who do not, even when raw intelligence is equivalent. The implication is profound: intelligence alone is not enough; it must be directed by awareness. The same holds true outside classrooms. Leaders, artists, and scientists who cultivate reflective awareness often make bolder yet wiser decisions, precisely because they are attuned not only to their thoughts but also to the reliability of those thoughts.

Yet there is a shadow side. Metacognition can slip into hyper-vigilance, a constant monitoring of one's own mind that edges into paralysis. The trick is not to use it as a whip but as a compass. The goal is not endless scrutiny, but the cultivation of a subtle alertness: enough distance to question, enough trust to act. Balancing observation and participation—knowing when to step back and when to immerse—is the art of a mature mind.

Philosophically, metacognition raises unsettling questions. If I can think about my thoughts, am I separate from them? Where, then, is the "I"? Am I the thinker, the observer, or something that contains both? Different traditions answer differently: some suggest that the true self is the witness, others that the very act of questioning reveals the illusion of a fixed self altogether. Whatever one's conclusion, the exercise itself illuminates a truth: the mind is not a monolith but a layered process, capable of turning its gaze inward and reshaping itself through awareness.

The practical stakes, however, are immediate. Without metacognition, anger flares unchecked, decisions are made on autopilot, and patterns of self-sabotage repeat endlessly. With it, a pause appears. That pause is not empty; it is space enough to ask whether another response is possible. In that pause lies the difference between lashing out and listening, between rushing into a decision and considering its consequences, between being swept along by chatter and gently guiding it toward clarity.

And so we return to the theatre. The mind will always perform, its stage crowded with characters and its script constantly rewriting itself. Metacognition is the act of stepping into the audience, not to escape the play but to see it for what it is. Once you can do that, the question becomes: how do you wish to respond? Will you rewrite the script, shift the stage lighting, or simply watch with equanimity? The curtain has already risen; the performance is under way. What changes is whether you are trapped in the role or awake to the fact that you are, at the same time, the watcher.

The Observer's Seat

On a crowded commuter train, a young woman sits staring out of the window. Her face is still, but inside her mind a storm rages: Did she say the wrong thing at yesterday's meeting? Why hasn't her friend replied to that message? What if she never gets the promotion she wants? To anyone watching, she is just another passenger; to herself, she is caught in an unrelenting theatre of thought. Then something subtle happens: she notices. Instead of following the thread of the story, she recognises it as a story. For a brief moment, she is no longer the anxious protagonist but the audience—watching the script unfold with a certain detachment. In that instant, the storm eases. She has discovered, however fleetingly, the observer's seat.

This paradox—that peace lies not in controlling our thoughts but in observing them—has been recognised in traditions as old as the Upanishads and as contemporary as cognitive science. We are conditioned to believe that freedom comes from silencing the mind, yet the first true step is humbler and more radical: noticing. To watch the flow of thoughts without being carried away by them is to reclaim authority over one's attention. It is not suppression; it is perspective.

Neuroscience has begun to map what ancient practitioners long intuited. Functional MRI scans reveal that when people practise mindfulness—the disciplined act of observing present-moment experience without judgement—activity in the brain's default mode network decreases. This is the same network implicated in self-referential rumination. By occupying the observer's stance, the mind's endless loops soften. What once felt like a binding reality reveals itself as transient neural activity, no more substantial than passing weather.

The challenge, of course, lies in the practice. Observing thoughts sounds deceptively simple, but it cuts against habit. Our default is immersion: a thought arises, and we become it. "I will fail" is not recognised as a thought but experienced as truth. The observer's seat introduces a subtle but profound shift: *There is a thought of failure.* This small insertion—naming the thought as an event rather than an identity—creates space. Space in which alternative responses can appear. Space in which one can breathe.

Practical methods for cultivating this stance range from meditation cushions to boardrooms. A classic exercise asks one to imagine thoughts as leaves floating down a stream. Each arises, drifts past, and disappears, without need to clutch or resist. Another, drawn from Acceptance and Commitment Therapy, encourages repeating a troubling phrase—"I am inadequate, I am inadequate"—until it loses its sting and is revealed for what it is: sounds, words, nothing more. Both techniques build the same capacity: to watch rather than be consumed.

Yet this shift is not merely a psychological trick; it carries ethical weight. The ability to step into the observer's seat allows us to pause before reacting in anger, to question whether our assumptions about others are fair, to detect the distortions that turn difference into threat. In this sense, observation is not withdrawal but responsibility. It is the pause that enables wisdom to intervene where impulse once ruled.

The cultural implications are equally striking. In societies where busyness is valorised and productivity is equated with worth, the observer's seat offers quiet resistance. To step back from one's thoughts is to step back from the compulsions of the marketplace. It is to remember that identity is not the sum of one's output or anxieties but something subtler, less easily commodified. For this reason, mindfulness programmes have found traction not only in clinics but also in schools, corporations, and even the military: attention is power, and observing attention is mastery.

Philosophically, the observer's seat unsettles the very notion of self. If I can observe my thoughts, am I identical with them? Or am I the witnessing awareness in which they appear? Some traditions answer by affirming a deeper self, the silent witness behind the noise. Others suggest the very distinction is illusory—that the self is nothing more than the interplay of thoughts and the awareness that notices them. Wherever one lands, the act of observing stretches identity beyond its usual confines, inviting us to inhabit a wider field of consciousness.

And yet, the observer's seat is not a place of escape. It is not about detaching from life but about engaging more fully with it. When one learns to watch anger without being consumed, one is freer to respond with clarity. When one recognises fear as a passing mental event, courage becomes possible. Far from numbing us, observation sharpens our capacity to act. It transforms life from a script we are trapped in to a play we can consciously perform.

The image of sitting in the audience of one's own mind is both reassuring and disquieting. Reassuring, because it reminds us that we are not condemned to drown in our thoughts; disquieting, because it forces us to admit that much of what we take as "reality" is a projection we can choose to watch differently. The question, then, is not whether thoughts will arise—they always will—but whether we will notice them with enough distance to choose our stance.

That commuter on the train, staring at the blur of buildings, discovered this truth by accident. You do not have to wait for accidents. The observer's seat is always available—an invitation to watch the mind with curiosity, to refuse its tyranny, and to glimpse the freedom that lies in awareness itself. Whether we accept that invitation is another matter. The mind will speak regardless. What changes everything is whether we are lost in its voice, or awake to the fact that we are listening.

Cognitive Defusion

A thought can undo a person. Not a violent act, nor a devastating event, but a single phrase whispered in the privacy of one's own mind: *I am not good enough*. Spoken silently, it coils itself around identity, tightening until it feels indistinguishable from truth. Yet, consider this paradox: the thought is nothing more than electrical impulses sparking across neurons, a passing pattern of language and memory. Why then do we treat it as an immutable reality? The answer lies in fusion—the mind's tendency to glue us to the literal content of its messages. The antidote, developed in contemporary psychology and honed across contemplative traditions, is cognitive defusion: the art of loosening this glue, of stepping back to see thoughts for what they are—fleeting events, not facts.

Acceptance and Commitment Therapy (ACT), the framework where the term "cognitive defusion" gained prominence, begins with a deceptively simple premise:

suffering often arises not from painful experiences themselves but from the way we entangle with our thoughts about them. A man rejected in love may be wounded, but when his mind insists *I am unlovable,* the pain calcifies into identity. A woman facing uncertainty at work may feel anxious, but when the thought *I will fail* becomes unquestioned gospel, anxiety expands into paralysis. Fusion is this unquestioned acceptance; defusion is the liberation of seeing.

To grasp this distinction, one must first understand the trickery of language. Human beings are unique in their capacity for symbolic thought. Words do not merely describe reality—they create it. Tell a child often enough that she is "lazy" and she may grow into the role, not because of her innate tendencies but because the label ossified into her sense of self. Defusion interrupts this spell. By learning to notice the word *lazy* as just a sound, a symbol, a thought produced by the mind, its hypnotic hold loosens. She is no longer imprisoned by the label; she can act in ways that disprove it.

One of the most elegant exercises from ACT illustrates this principle. Take the phrase "I am worthless." When repeated slowly, again and again, aloud or silently, the meaning begins to crumble. The words detach from the weight they once carried and become sounds, almost absurd in their repetition. What once felt like a crushing verdict reveals itself as a construction—letters, syllables, vibrations. This is cognitive defusion in practice: stripping a thought of its false authority by exposing its mechanics.

Another method involves inserting a simple preface: *I am having the thought that….* Instead of saying "I am going to fail," one reframes it as "I am having the thought that I am going to fail." That small linguistic wedge shifts perspective from fusion to observation. The thought is no longer the self but an object in awareness. With practice, one might even extend the phrase: *I notice that I am having the thought that I am going to fail.* Each added layer of distance pries the thinker further from the grip of the thought.

Of course, defusion is not about banishing thoughts or battling them into silence. To attempt that is to strengthen their hold, much as trying not to think of a pink elephant almost guarantees its presence in the mind. Instead, defusion treats thoughts as background noise, inevitable but non-binding. The mind can shout *You are weak* while the body continues forward, acting in alignment with deeper values. Defusion creates choice: the ability to act not according to the dictates of the thought but according to what matters most.

The practical consequences of this are profound. In clinical settings, defusion techniques have helped those with obsessive-compulsive disorder, depression, and anxiety disorders regain mobility in life. Rather than waiting for intrusive thoughts to disappear—a wait that can stretch into years—patients learn to carry them lightly, treating them as passing weather. Outside therapy rooms, professionals use defusion to steady themselves before high-stakes presentations, athletes before competitions, even parents in moments of domestic stress. The inner narrator can scream, but one need not obey.

Philosophically, defusion forces us to reconsider the boundaries of self. If thoughts are not identical with "me," then who am I? Am I the thinker, the thought, or the witness behind both? Cognitive science tends towards pragmatic answers, emphasising the functional value of defusion in reducing distress and increasing flexibility. Contemplative traditions, by contrast, take the insight further, suggesting that the very idea of a fixed self dissolves under close observation. Defusion thus sits at the crossroads of psychology and philosophy, offering both practical relief and existential provocation.

And yet, defusion is not without its tensions. Can too much distance from thoughts risk apathy or detachment? If one learns to treat even the thought *I should help* as mere mental noise, what anchors moral action? Advocates of ACT would argue that defusion is never practised in isolation but always alongside values clarification. It is not about ignoring thoughts wholesale but about discerning which align with one's chosen life directions and which merely sabotage. Still, the tension remains fruitful, reminding us that every liberation carries responsibilities.

To sit in defusion is to experience a quiet revolution: the shift from *I am my thoughts* to *I have thoughts*. This shift is not dramatic in appearance—no sudden epiphanies, no lightning bolts—but its cumulative effects are radical. The woman once paralysed by self-doubt still hears the whisper of failure, but now she recognises it as just that—a whisper, not a command. The man once defined by rejection still feels the sting of memory, but now he sees the thought *I am unlovable* as precisely that—a thought, not a prophecy.

Perhaps the greater paradox is this: liberation does not come from silencing the mind but from watching it speak. To separate from thought is to step into freedom. But the question that remains, and it is one that each reader must eventually confront, is this: once you see your thoughts for what they are, what will you do with the space that opens up?

From Awareness to Choice

A heated argument, a harsh email, a cutting remark—moments like these reveal the difference between living at the mercy of our thoughts and emotions and reclaiming agency through awareness. Imagine someone criticises your work in a meeting. Before awareness can intervene, your body floods with adrenaline, your mind races with defensive retorts, and words escape that you later regret. Yet if, in that fleeting instant, awareness catches the spark—*I notice I am angry, I notice the urge to retaliate*—the outcome shifts. A pause opens. A choice appears. What was once an automatic reaction becomes a deliberate response. This is the promise of metacognition: the transformation of mental noise into clarity, and of reflex into choice.

The paradox is stark. Human beings pride themselves on free will, yet much of daily life unfolds on autopilot. We react before we reflect, habitually pulled by scripts laid down through evolution, culture, and personal history. Anger begets angry words; worry begets avoidance; shame begets silence. Neuroscience underscores this point: the brain's fast emotional circuits often precede conscious deliberation by fractions of a second. We are, in many ways, predictably mechanical. And yet, through metacognition—the act of noticing thought as thought—we carve out the space in which genuine freedom resides.

This pause is not passive. It is an active disruption of the cycle where stimulus reflexively dictates response. In cognitive behavioural terms, awareness interrupts the chain linking *trigger* → *thought* → *feeling* → *action*. With practice, that interruption lengthens, and within it, new possibilities emerge. The critic's remark may still sting, but instead of immediate retaliation, one might choose curiosity ("What exactly does this feedback reveal?") or restraint ("I will reflect before responding"). Awareness does not erase emotion; it recontextualises it, converting raw reactivity into informed choice.

Examples abound in everyday life. The professional facing a daunting presentation feels the familiar wave of anxiety. Fused with thought, she might cancel, procrastinate, or deliver poorly while gripped by fear. With metacognitive awareness, however, she recognises: *I am having the thought that I will embarrass myself*. That recognition creates a gap. She can proceed, still nervous, but guided not by fear's dictate but by her value of growth or her commitment to her team. Similarly, the parent exhausted after a long day may feel the automatic urge to snap at a child's misbehaviour. Awareness of the rising urge provides a beat to breathe, softening the reply from sharp reprimand to measured correction. The shift is subtle yet transformative: life ceases to be purely reactive, becoming instead a field of conscious engagement.

Philosophically, this pause lies at the heart of many wisdom traditions. The Stoics spoke of *prohairesis*—the inner faculty of choice—distinguishing what lies within our control from what does not. Buddhist teachings describe the cultivation of "bare attention," observing thought and sensation without grasping or aversion. In modern neuroscience, studies of mindfulness training show strengthened prefrontal regulation over limbic impulses, literally rewiring the brain to sustain the pause before reaction. Across traditions and disciplines, the insight converges: awareness precedes freedom.

Still, the practice is far from easy. The pull of habit is immense, and the mind, left unattended, defaults to speed and certainty. Psychologists describe "cognitive load" and "ego depletion"—states in which mental resources are drained, leaving us more prone to knee-jerk responses. In such conditions, awareness requires deliberate cultivation. Simple practices—a breath before speaking, a brief mental label ("anger," "fear," "urge")—can strengthen the muscle of pausing. Over time, the pause lengthens from milliseconds to moments, enough to alter the trajectory of decisions, relationships, and lives.

The implications extend beyond the personal. In leadership, the difference between impulsive reaction and reflective choice can determine whether a team spirals into conflict or finds constructive solutions. In social discourse, awareness offers a buffer against the contagion of outrage, enabling dialogue where there might otherwise be division. Even in global contexts, one might argue that humanity's capacity to pause—to reflect before deploying technology, consuming resources, or retaliating in conflict—will shape the fate of civilisations. From awareness to choice is not merely an individual skill; it is a collective imperative.

Yet this raises a deeper question: if awareness grants choice, how do we decide wisely? Awareness alone is insufficient. Once we notice a thought, we must orient ourselves by values, goals, and ethics. Otherwise, awareness risks becoming a detached spectator sport, seeing but never steering. The pause, therefore, is a hinge. It opens the door, but we must still step through. Choice, at its best, aligns with what we care about most deeply—not with the loudest voice in the mind, but with the quiet compass of principle and purpose.

The image is simple yet profound: a pause as a fulcrum. On one side lies the inertia of old patterns; on the other, the possibility of deliberate direction. To cultivate metacognition is to strengthen this fulcrum, to make the pivot from noise to clarity more accessible, more reliable, more humane. In time, one begins to sense the extraordinary hidden within the ordinary: the microsecond pause before a word, the half-breath before an action, the still moment before decision. These are the sites where lives are shaped.

And yet, a tension remains. If every pause holds choice, what do we do with that responsibility? To be aware is to carry the burden of freedom, to confront the fact that we cannot always blame habit, impulse, or conditioning. The pause hands us the reins. But will we grip them firmly, guiding our lives toward what matters, or will we let them slip, surrendering again to reflex? This is the challenge metacognition places before us: once you learn to create the pause, what choices will you dare to make?

Chapter 6
Training Attention Like a Muscle

In 2007, neuroscientists at Stanford conducted an experiment that should have ended the myth of multitasking once and for all. They brought in heavy media users—people who proudly juggled emails, social feeds, music streams, and word documents simultaneously—and put them to the test. The results were embarrassing. These self-proclaimed masters of multitasking performed worse than their single-tasking peers on virtually every measure: memory, task-switching, even the ability to filter out irrelevant information. Far from being cognitive athletes, their minds were scattered, weakened by constant switching. The study captured something most of us sense but rarely admit: what feels like efficiency is often a slow erosion of clarity.

Consider the modern office, or the ordinary smartphone screen. Notifications flutter, emails ping, tabs multiply, and one's attention is pulled in a dozen directions at once. It feels active, even productive, but underneath lies fragmentation. Attention splinters into shards, and what should be a steady beam of focus becomes a flickering, unreliable light. The paradox is stark: in a time when mental labour is more prized than ever, we systematically undermine the very faculty that makes it possible. The cost is not only in missed deadlines or poor concentration; it is in a diminished capacity to inhabit our lives fully.

This chapter argues for a radical reframing. Attention is not an infinite, passive resource to be squandered; it is a finite, trainable capacity, closer to a muscle than a spotlight. Like any muscle, it grows stronger with deliberate exercise and weaker when neglected. The practices of ancient contemplatives—monks counting breaths in monasteries, sages cultivating stillness—now find empirical support in neuroscience labs. Regular training of attention thickens grey matter in regions linked to executive control, enhances working memory, and reduces susceptibility to distraction. What once seemed mystical is now measurable.

The heart of the practice is deceptively simple: single-point focus. Whether on the breath, a candle flame, a musical note, or the swing of a golf club, the act of steadying attention on one chosen object counteracts the brain's tendency to wander. Studies show the average mind drifts nearly half the time; mindfulness trains it to return, again and again, until focus becomes less a fleeting accident and more a cultivated habit. This is not about suppression of thought, but about learning to sustain and redirect attention, as one might guide a restless horse.

Yet training attention does not require retreat to a mountaintop or hours of silent meditation. Micro-moments scattered through the day—the deliberate noticing of breath before a meeting, the slow steps of a mindful walk between tasks, the single sip of coffee tasted fully—can accumulate into profound change. These brief exercises create anchor points in the storm of daily life, reminders that attention can be reclaimed in seconds. The metaphor of the muscle applies here too: small repetitions, consistently performed, yield strength.

Athletes, musicians, and surgeons exemplify this principle. The archer who blocks out crowd noise, the pianist who surrenders entirely to the keys, the surgeon who operates for hours with unwavering steadiness—all embody attention trained to its peak. But what is often overlooked are the rituals and environments that support such feats: quiet practice rooms, disciplined routines, intentional removal of distraction. Focus, they reveal, is not only about internal control but about constructing external conditions that protect and sustain it.

The challenge, of course, is that our environment is rarely designed for stillness. The attention economy profits from distraction, capturing our gaze to sell it. Devices are engineered to trigger craving; platforms thrive on fragmented engagement. To reclaim attention is therefore an act of resistance as well as of self-care. It is to declare that the mind will not be hijacked endlessly, that focus is too precious to be auctioned to the highest bidder.

What, then, does it mean to train attention in such a world? Is it enough to practise in brief intervals, or must we fundamentally reshape our relationship with technology, productivity, and rest? Can we design lives that both accommodate constant demands and protect the sanctity of focus? These questions frame the task ahead. For at stake is more than efficiency—it is our ability to think deeply, connect fully, and live deliberately in a distracted age.

The Myth of Multitasking

In the late 1990s, as Silicon Valley began exporting the gospel of efficiency, multitasking became its catechism. Job adverts promised fast-paced environments where candidates must "juggle priorities." Productivity books urged readers to master "parallel processing." Executives wore their ability to field emails during meetings, reply to texts while commuting, and brainstorm during conference calls as badges of honour. To be busy was to be important; to be able to do five things at once was to be indispensable.

And yet, under scrutiny, this cultural boast begins to collapse. Neuroscience has long established that the human brain cannot truly perform two demanding cognitive tasks simultaneously. What feels like multitasking is in fact rapid task-switching—attention shuttling back and forth, leaving a trail of half-formed thoughts and diminished output. Like a computer with too many windows open, the mind slows as it attempts to update each program in turn. What is presented as mastery is often inefficiency masquerading as competence.

Cognitive load theory provides the scientific underpinning of this illusion. Our working memory—the mental notepad on which we hold and manipulate information—is both limited and fragile. Overload it, and performance degrades. Every time attention switches, the brain incurs a cost: a reset delay, a reorientation period, and a brief vulnerability to distraction. Researchers at the University of London even found that constant multitasking can reduce cognitive performance to the level of someone who has missed an entire night's sleep. The toll is not metaphorical—it is measurable.

Consider the surgeon whose focus drifts between patient and pager, or the driver glancing between the road and a buzzing phone. The stakes here are not just efficiency but safety and precision. Studies consistently reveal that distraction—even momentary—leads to errors that single-taskers avoid. A few seconds lost in reorienting can be the difference between accuracy and accident. The modern workplace, by celebrating divided attention, builds conditions ripe for avoidable mistakes.

There is, of course, nuance. Not all multitasking is equally damaging. Folding laundry while listening to a podcast, or jogging while reflecting on a problem, can be benign or even beneficial. These combinations pair one low-demand, almost automatic activity with another that requires thought. The problem arises when two cognitively taxing tasks compete for the same limited pool of attention. Reading an email while participating in a meeting, or drafting a report while fielding instant messages, asks the brain to split its spotlight. Inevitably, something falls into shadow.

Philosophically, the myth of multitasking also speaks to a deeper cultural unease. In societies that equate self-worth with productivity, the pressure to be constantly occupied is immense. To do one thing at a time may appear lazy, indulgent, or insufficient. Multitasking flatters the ego—it suggests not only efficiency but superiority, a mind agile enough to outperform the ordinary. Yet, the data humbles this illusion. Far from elevating us, the practice diminishes our capacity for depth, robbing us of the very excellence we pursue.

There is another irony here: the human mind is most creative not when overloaded, but when given space. The painter absorbed in brushstrokes, the scientist lost in a single equation, the musician immersed in a score—these are states of flow, where attention narrows and performance expands. Multitasking fractures the conditions required for such flow, replacing immersion with constant surface-skimming. We become generalists of distraction rather than specialists of presence.

Some companies are beginning to awaken to this truth. Tech firms now experiment with "focus time" blocks, universities teach students strategies for monotasking, and productivity apps ironically sell what their industry once eroded: the capacity to concentrate. But even these solutions struggle against the wider tide of a culture wired for interruptions—email alerts, message badges, news pings—all designed to fracture attention for profit. The battle is not only internal but systemic.

So the question lingers: if multitasking is a myth, why do we cling to it so stubbornly? Perhaps because it feeds two simultaneous hungers—the desire to feel busy and the desire to feel capable. To relinquish it is to admit our limits, to accept that depth requires narrowing rather than widening. And yet, in that narrowing lies the possibility of true mastery.

What might happen if we stopped venerating the juggler and started admiring the craftsman, the one who attends fully to a single act? What kind of clarity, creativity, and humanity might re-emerge if we resisted the lure of fractured focus? The myth of multitasking has shaped modern life; dismantling it will demand courage not just in our habits but in our values. The path forward begins with a humbler but far more radical act: the willingness to do one thing well, and nothing else.

The Practice of Single-Point Focus

In an age where distractions clamour for our attention with relentless persistence, the simple act of focusing on one thing seems almost radical. Picture a monk seated in a quiet monastery, his gaze resting steadily on the flame of a candle. Hours pass, yet he remains, breathing slowly, absorbed in the flickering light. For most of us, holding attention for even a minute feels arduous, our minds leaping restlessly from task to notification, from thought to memory. The paradox is striking: never has the human capacity for attention been more valuable, and never has it been under such siege.

The human brain was not designed for endless fragmentation. It evolved to scan, to shift, to notice what changed in the environment as a matter of survival. Yet it also evolved the capacity for absorption: the hunter tracking the faintest trail, the artisan shaping wood with steady hands, the child rapt in play. These states of immersion—moments when consciousness narrows and deepens—represent some of the most rewarding experiences available to us. They arise not by chance but through cultivation, and at their heart lies the discipline of single-point focus.

Mindfulness and meditation traditions have long recognised the power of training attention. Anchoring awareness to a single object—be it the breath, a sound, a visual form, or even a repeated phrase—serves as a kind of mental weightlifting. Each time the mind wanders and is gently returned, the neural pathways of attention are strengthened. Cognitive scientists have observed this through brain imaging: regions involved in executive control, particularly the prefrontal cortex, grow more efficient with practice. What might feel like the humble act of noticing an inhale is, in fact, rewiring the architecture of awareness.

One of the most accessible forms is breath meditation. At first, it seems deceptively simple: sit comfortably, close your eyes, and attend to the rising and falling of the breath. Within moments, thoughts intrude—reminders, worries, plans. The novice meditator often concludes they are failing. Yet this is precisely the point: the practice is not about maintaining unbroken focus but about recognising distraction and returning. Each return is a rep, each rep a strengthening of the attentional muscle. The flame of concentration brightens incrementally, often imperceptibly, until over time the capacity for presence becomes more stable.

Case studies from clinical settings reinforce this. Patients suffering from anxiety and depression, when taught mindfulness practices, often report not just relief from symptoms but a shift in how they relate to their thoughts. Where once attention was hijacked by rumination, they begin to notice a gap between stimulus and response. That gap—the pause—provides room for deliberate choice rather than automatic reaction. Single-point focus is not escapism; it is the cultivation of sovereignty over one's own mental life.

The practice extends beyond the meditation cushion. A surgeon, for instance, must hold unwavering attention during an operation. An Olympic archer steadies their focus on the target despite the noise of the crowd. A novelist enters a flow state, losing all sense of time while absorbed in the rhythm of language. Though the domains differ, the principle is the same: single-point focus transforms performance because it channels the full force of consciousness into a chosen act.

Still, there is resistance. Many find the idea of sustained attention intimidating, equating it with rigidity or denial of spontaneity. Yet paradoxically, it is through focus that freedom expands. By committing to one thing at a time, we liberate ourselves from the tyranny of partial engagement. Fragmented attention produces a scattered self; concentrated attention yields a coherent one. The choice to rest the mind on a single object is not a narrowing of life but a deepening of it.

There is also a cultural tension worth noting. Modern economies thrive on distraction—advertising, social media, notifications—each designed to capture and commodify attention. To train single-point focus is, in a sense, an act of quiet rebellion. It asserts that the most valuable resource is not time or money but attention itself. By directing it consciously, we reclaim what the noise of the world seeks to fracture.

Some traditions recommend starting small: focusing on a single sip of tea, a few mindful steps while walking, the texture of a single sound. These micro-practices gradually extend the capacity for concentration into daily life. Others prefer structured meditation sessions, building endurance much like training for a marathon. Both paths converge on the same truth: focus, like any skill, strengthens through repetition and patience.

Yet a question lingers, unresolved: if single-point focus is so potent, why do we resist it? Perhaps because it confronts us with the simplicity of the present, stripping away the comfort of distraction. To sit with one thing is to face ourselves, unbuffered by the noise that usually shields us. It is here that single-point focus reveals its deepest challenge and its greatest promise: it is not just about productivity or calm, but about learning to inhabit life more fully.

What might change if we each learned to rest in that steadiness—not for hours in a monastery, but for moments scattered through our hurried days? Could single-point focus become not merely a technique but a way of moving through the world, deliberate and unhurried, in defiance of its constant pull toward distraction? The answer lies not in abstraction but in practice, one breath, one step, one act of attention at a time.

Micro-Moments of Awareness

Consider the paradox: we plan elaborate holidays, weekend retreats, or sabbaticals in pursuit of peace, yet often overlook the seconds scattered throughout each day that could offer the same reprieve. A breath between emails, the pause at a red light, the stillness before answering a phone call—moments so small they slip beneath awareness. Yet within them lies a hidden reservoir of stillness, available without cost or calendar, if only we learn to notice.

One morning in a bustling London hospital, a surgeon was observed standing utterly still before entering the operating theatre. He was not checking his notes or revising procedure details. He simply closed his eyes for three breaths. Colleagues later asked about the habit, and his answer was straightforward: *"If I am not steady, the knife is not steady."* That ritual of pause—barely thirty seconds long—was his anchor. In a profession where attention wavers at the cost of lives, micro-moments of awareness are not indulgences but necessities.

What this surgeon demonstrates on a grand stage applies just as much in everyday life. The human nervous system thrives on rhythm, not unbroken acceleration. Yet modern culture rewards momentum and treats pauses with suspicion. The result is a kind of cognitive suffocation: endless input, no time to metabolise. Just as the body requires oxygen between heartbeats, the mind requires intervals of awareness amidst its constant firing. Without them, clarity and resilience degrade.

Micro-moments of awareness are deceptively simple: brief, intentional shifts of attention back to the present. They are not designed to empty the mind but to stabilise it, like a sailor adjusting the sails rather than fighting the storm. Research on mindfulness has shown that even short practices—ten seconds of breath awareness, a single minute of body scanning—can measurably reduce stress markers such as cortisol. Small doses accumulate, altering not just mood but baseline attentional control.

Examples abound in practical life. Consider the commuter who uses the stop at each station not to check their phone but to register the sensation of sitting, the texture of sound around them, the cadence of their own breathing. Over weeks, this transforms the commute from dead time into training time. Or the parent who, before responding to a child's question, silently inhales and exhales once, creating a fraction of space between impulse and reply. These are not grand meditative sessions but brief recalibrations of awareness—threads of calm woven into the fabric of ordinary living.

The principle is ancient. Zen monks sweep courtyards grain by grain, not because the ground is particularly dirty but because attention itself is being refined. Thích Nhất Hạnh often taught "mindful walking" in which each step, however small, was a complete event. Modern neuroscience validates these practices: studies on interoception—the awareness of internal bodily states—show that momentary attention to breath or heartbeat strengthens neural circuits linking the insula and prefrontal cortex, enhancing both self-regulation and resilience to stress.

Yet micro-moments face cultural resistance. Our economies monetise attention; to withdraw it, even briefly, feels like rebellion. A worker pausing at their desk for five seconds of silent breathing may appear idle in an office culture equating busyness with worth. The irony is stark: the very practices that sharpen focus and efficiency are often mistaken for inefficiency. To reclaim them requires a reframing: stillness is not absence of work but optimisation of it.

There is also a psychological tension. Many fear that stopping, even briefly, will allow buried worries to surface. To be quiet for a minute is to encounter one's own mind unfiltered, and that can feel uncomfortable. But discomfort here is not a sign of failure; it is the beginning of awareness. The practice of micro-moments does not eliminate intrusive thoughts but teaches us to see them arise and pass without panic. Over time, these glimpses accumulate into trust: the mind is noisy, yes, but it need not dictate every response.

Practical exercises need not be complicated. One method is the "breath check": at natural pauses in the day—before sending an email, entering a meeting, or taking a sip of water—direct attention to a single inhalation and exhalation. Another is the "five senses reset": notice one thing you can see, hear, feel, smell, and taste. Each practice lasts under a minute, yet each plants a flag of presence in the rush of time. These flags, once frequent enough, begin to reorient the landscape of a day.

The deeper significance of micro-moments lies not only in stress relief but in identity. When we insert pauses, we discover ourselves not as the stream of tasks, roles, or thoughts, but as the observer capable of stepping back. This shift, repeated daily, nurtures self-awareness in its most practical form. From there arises a subtle but profound freedom: the ability to choose our engagement rather than being perpetually pulled by momentum.

And so the question arises: what would a day look like if punctuated not by digital alerts but by intentional pauses? How might the quality of thought, decision, and relationship change if awareness were trained in fragments rather than reserved for retreats? The answer cannot be given in theory; it must be lived, moment by moment, breath by breath. Perhaps the great transformation of mental life begins not with hours of discipline, but with seconds reclaimed.

Sustaining Focus in a Distracted World

A world-class violinist once confessed that the most difficult part of her practice was not mastering the technical intricacies of Bach's sonatas but defending ninety uninterrupted minutes from the encroachment of the world. The challenge was not the music itself but the maintenance of silence around it—the clearing of space where her attention could settle, unbroken, long enough for something extraordinary to unfold. Her predicament mirrors our own: the modern scarcity is not talent, information, or opportunity, but the ability to sustain focus amid constant intrusion.

The paradox is striking. We live in an age where human beings perform neurosurgery while machines breathe for the patient, where athletes execute flawless routines under crushing pressure, where composers draw symphonies from the quiet recesses of the mind. Yet most people struggle to read a single article without checking their phone. The same capacity for deep concentration that allows surgeons, musicians, and athletes to reach the apex of human achievement is available to all, but it must be protected and trained with as much discipline as any physical skill.

Athletes understand this instinctively. A sprinter at the starting line is not merely waiting for the gun; she is inhabiting a cocoon of focus, filtering out the roar of the stadium. Sports psychologists teach rituals—tying laces in a particular order, repeating a mantra, or visualising the race—because these micro-acts signal to the brain: now, attend. The rituals are less about superstition than about conditioning the nervous system into readiness. Neuroscience supports this: consistent pre-performance routines reduce variability in attentional control, making focus more reliable under pressure.

Musicians adopt parallel strategies. Glenn Gould, the famously eccentric pianist, insisted on a specific chair worn almost to collapse, claiming it grounded his playing. Cellists breathe with the bow, synchronising bodily rhythm with sound to sustain flow. These idiosyncratic rituals create continuity between practice and performance, stabilising attention in environments that might otherwise be saturated with nerves, distractions, or expectations. The lesson transcends the concert hall: sustained focus requires not just willpower but environmental scaffolding.

Nowhere is this more apparent than in surgery. Studies on operating teams show that the most successful surgeons are those who standardise their environment to the point of ritual: the same music, the same order of instruments, the same quiet before incision. These practices are not quirks of personality but defences against distraction. In an age where the beeps of monitors and the urgency of pagers abound, such rituals carve out islands of control. Focus is preserved not by exclusion of chaos but by designing an inner and outer setting resilient to it.

Outside these elite contexts, sustaining focus may appear more difficult. Our offices and homes are saturated with alerts, emails, and headlines engineered to fracture attention. Yet the principles remain the same. Focus is best preserved through deliberate design. This may mean arranging the physical environment—closing unnecessary tabs, silencing notifications, or even working in spaces associated only with specific tasks. It may also mean building rituals that mark the transition into deep work: a cup of tea brewed the same way, a notebook opened at the same desk, a few breaths to steady the mind.

Philosophically, this insistence on ritual reflects an ancient truth: attention is not an inexhaustible resource. The Stoics counselled morning preparation and evening reflection, not as piety but as architecture for focus. Buddhist monastics have long paired chants and gestures with meditation to stabilise awareness. What athletes, surgeons, and musicians rediscover in their own practices is something these traditions intuited centuries ago—that focus is less an act of brute force than a cultivated rhythm of mind and environment.

Yet sustaining focus in a distracted world demands confronting a deeper tension. Distraction is not merely external; it is also internal. One can silence the phone, close the door, dim the lights, and still be besieged by the mind's noise. Here rituals perform a dual role: they regulate the outer environment while anchoring the inner one. The sprinter's mantra, the violinist's bowing exercises, the surgeon's breath—all act as bridges between external readiness and internal clarity. In ordinary life, we too can adopt such bridges: a consistent journaling practice, a meditation bell before work, or simply a repeated phrase that brings attention back when it drifts.

Sustaining focus, then, is not about eliminating distraction altogether—an impossible task—but about engineering conditions in which attention can thrive despite it. It is about transforming the world from an adversary into a collaborator, where cues, spaces, and rhythms all conspire to protect the fragile flame of concentration.

The open question remains: in an economy built on the harvesting of attention, can we reclaim enough of it to live not just reactively but deliberately? The answer will not arrive from another app or another layer of noise. It will be forged in rituals, environments, and habits that honour the mind's need for depth. The practices of athletes, musicians, and surgeons remind us that sustained focus is not an accident but an art—one that must be cultivated if we wish not only to perform but to live fully.

Chapter 7
Rewriting the Loops

The human mind has an extraordinary capacity to build entire worlds out of words no one else will ever hear. A single stray thought—"What if I fail?"—can spiral into a full-blown prediction of humiliation, financial ruin, or permanent loss of respect. None of it has occurred, yet the body responds as though it already has: the heart races, the muscles tense, the breath shortens. In these moments we are not reacting to reality but to a private narrative, crafted by our own inner narrator, rehearsed so often it feels indisputable. The most insidious part is not that the story is false, but that it is *unexamined*.

Consider a professional delivering a presentation. Midway through, they stumble on a word. Instantly, an inner loop ignites: *They think I'm incompetent. I've blown it. I should never have agreed to this.* The audience, however, registers barely a flicker. The distortion lies not in the stumble but in the interpretation. These loops of thought—automatic, repetitive, self-reinforcing—shape not just what we feel in a given moment but who we believe ourselves to be.

Cognitive science has shown that the brain is a prediction machine, but what it often predicts is failure, rejection, or danger, even in contexts where none exists. Psychologists call these distortions: catastrophising, mind-reading, overgeneralisation. What unites them is their rigidity. They present possibilities as inevitabilities, speculation as fact.

And left unchecked, they accumulate into self-concepts: not just *I made a mistake* but *I am a failure*. The raw loops of survival anxiety become the architecture of identity.

This chapter examines how such loops can be caught, challenged, and ultimately reshaped. The process is not about silencing the mind or manufacturing positivity but about scrutinising the mechanics of thought with the same precision we might apply to a scientific claim or legal argument. Evidence-based reframing, a cornerstone of cognitive behavioural therapy, invites us to test our assumptions against reality: What evidence supports this belief? What evidence contradicts it? What is the cost of continuing to think this way? Such questions pry open the loop, introducing flexibility where rigidity once ruled.

Language plays a pivotal role. Words are not neutral labels; they are tools that can inflame or soothe, constrict or expand. Saying "I am worthless" embeds identity in a passing feeling, while rephrasing to "I feel inadequate right now" creates space between self and state. The difference may appear semantic, but its psychological impact is profound. Subtle shifts in phrasing alter how emotions are processed, how behaviour follows, and how loops are rewritten.

Just as physical strength grows with repeated practice, so too does mental flexibility. Cognitive restructuring is not a single breakthrough but a discipline, a willingness to return again and again to the inner theatre of thought, recognising distortions not as verdicts but as hypotheses. With repetition, the brain learns not only to challenge unhelpful patterns but to replace them with perspectives that are balanced, constructive, and responsive to reality.

The stakes are not trivial. A life dominated by unchecked loops is one of constant rehearsal for disasters that rarely arrive. A life shaped by rewoven loops is not devoid of struggle, but it is free from unnecessary imprisonment in self-created stories. The question this chapter leaves hanging is both practical and existential: if the loops in your head can be rewritten, then how much of who you take yourself to be is open to revision? The answer may determine not only how you think, but how you live.

Catching Cognitive Biases in Action

A university student receives an email from their supervisor with the subject line "Meeting Request." Within seconds, their stomach tightens. *I must have done something wrong. They've found a mistake in my work. Maybe they regret admitting me to the programme at all.* By the time the student clicks open the message, they have rehearsed scenarios of academic disgrace and expulsion. The actual email, however, is brief and neutral: "Let's catch up next week to discuss your progress."

This is how swiftly cognitive biases hijack perception. A routine event becomes an existential threat, not because of its content but because of the mind's interpretation. These distortions are not rare glitches; they are the default tendencies of an organ evolved for survival, not accuracy. The brain's genius lies in its ability to anticipate danger, but that same brilliance bends easily towards exaggeration, misattribution, and self-sabotage.

Consider the employee who receives constructive feedback during an annual review. The manager praises multiple achievements but adds one suggestion for improvement. By the end of the day, the employee recalls only the critique, replaying it until it swells into confirmation of deep inadequacy. This is *filtering,* a form of bias where negatives are magnified and positives discarded. Another worker, facing the same review, may interpret it differently—viewing the single criticism as evidence that perfection is expected and therefore unattainable. The same external stimulus, refracted through different biases, yields entirely different realities.

The cognitive distortions most commonly catalogued by psychologists read like a taxonomy of human misperception: catastrophising (leaping to the worst possible outcome), black-and-white thinking (dividing the world into absolutes), personalisation (assuming undue responsibility), mind-reading (imagining others' judgments), and emotional reasoning (believing feelings are facts). Each bias represents a shortcut—an attempt by the brain to impose certainty on ambiguity. Yet each shortcut narrows perspective, often closing off the very possibilities that would ease anxiety.

Take catastrophising. A late-night text from a partner goes unanswered. Within hours, the mind spins a story: *They're angry. The relationship is failing. I will end up alone.* The origin of the worry is understandable—humans are wired to maintain social bonds—but the leap from silence to catastrophe is disproportionate. What's striking is not the inaccuracy but the conviction: the imagined outcome feels as real as an external fact.

Or consider personalisation. A friend seems distant at a dinner. Instantly, the thought arises: *I must have offended them. I said something wrong.* Rarely does the first reflexive explanation run, *Perhaps they are tired, preoccupied, or unwell.* The self becomes the focal point of blame, not because evidence supports it but because the bias steers interpretation inwards. This habit of over-responsibility can corrode self-esteem and make ordinary interactions exhausting.

Biases do not operate only in private rumination; they influence collective narratives as well. Financial markets can swing on catastrophising, with investors extrapolating from a single datapoint to apocalyptic predictions. Political discourse thrives on black-and-white thinking, casting opponents as wholly good or wholly evil, obliterating nuance. Social media accelerates personalisation, where a lack of response to a message or post is read as intentional slight. The same mechanisms that shape a student's anxiety about an email shape global patterns of decision-making and conflict.

What makes these biases so difficult to catch is their camouflage. They present themselves not as guesses but as *truths*. When someone thinks, *They didn't reply—they must hate me,* the statement is felt as reality, not hypothesis. The practice of catching biases in action requires developing a second layer of awareness: to notice the leap from event to interpretation, to pause before assumption hardens into conviction.

A useful exercise is to map situations with three columns: the event, the automatic thought, and the possible distortions. For instance:
Event — Supervisor says, "We need to talk."
Automatic thought — "I'm about to be fired."
Possible distortion — Catastrophising, mind-reading.

Such mapping transforms the abstract notion of bias into a concrete pattern. Over time, the act of naming the distortion loosens its grip.

Philosophers have long recognised this gap between perception and reality. Epictetus, the Stoic teacher, wrote: "Men are disturbed not by things, but by the view which they take of them." Modern cognitive science echoes this: the distress is less in the event than in the interpretation. To catch biases in action is to stand at the threshold of that gap and observe how swiftly thought leaps to fill it.

Yet catching them is not the same as escaping them. A bias identified does not vanish; it resurfaces, dressed in subtler disguises. The challenge, then, is not to aspire to perfect neutrality but to cultivate vigilance. Awareness turns the distortion from dictator to suspect, from command to suggestion. The tension that remains is unresolved but vital: if the mind cannot be trusted to present reality faithfully, then how do we decide which thoughts deserve belief and which should be questioned?

That question—sharp, uncomfortable, and liberating—marks the beginning of cognitive freedom. It reminds us that while we cannot silence the biases altogether, we can learn to catch them mid-flight, to pause before they crystallise into unquestioned certainties. And in that pause lies the opening for choice.

Evidence-Based Reframing

A professional receives an email late at night: "We need to talk first thing tomorrow." Their heart rate spikes, their mind spins. *I've made a mistake. My job is at risk. They've lost confidence in me.* Sleep becomes impossible as catastrophic scenarios play out in vivid detail. The next morning, the meeting lasts five minutes. The boss simply wanted to discuss a new project.

This scene is not trivial. It illustrates how quickly the mind converts ambiguity into disaster. The email contained no threat, yet the narrative built around it felt unquestionable. Cognitive Behavioural Therapy (CBT) begins at this very point: not by denying the intensity of the thought, but by subjecting it to reality testing. What evidence supported the belief of looming failure? What alternative explanations existed? Once asked, these questions reveal how fragile the original certainty really was.

At the core of reframing lies a paradox: the brain is a prediction machine, constantly filling gaps with assumptions, yet those assumptions are rarely interrogated. Left unchecked, they calcify into biases, distortions, and self-fulfilling prophecies. Evidence-based reframing interrupts that cycle. It insists on slowing the process, bringing thought into dialogue with fact, and offering a more balanced interpretation of experience.

One of the simplest yet most profound tools of CBT is the thought record. Imagine writing down a distressing belief: *I am incompetent because I forgot one detail in the presentation.* Next, the evidence for: "I missed a point during the pitch." Then the evidence against: "The client still accepted the proposal. My colleagues supported my approach. I have successfully led other projects." Finally, a more balanced perspective: *I made a small mistake, but overall I am capable and effective.* What emerges is not rose-tinted optimism but proportion—a recalibration that rescues identity from the tyranny of a single flaw.

The power of reframing lies in its grounding. It does not demand blind positivity, which can be as distorting as negativity. Instead, it seeks accuracy. A thought like *Nobody likes me* collapses under scrutiny when contrasted with real evidence: friends who reach out, colleagues who collaborate, family members who show care. The mind may protest—*But they don't count, they're just being polite*—yet the exercise forces awareness of the selective blindness that fuels despair.

This practice also challenges cultural assumptions. Many societies valorise self-criticism, equating harsh internal judgement with humility or discipline. Yet research shows that excessive self-reproach undermines performance and resilience. Balanced reframing, far from excusing mediocrity, provides the clarity necessary to improve. It shifts the inner dialogue from *I am worthless* to *This part needs work, but I have succeeded elsewhere and can improve here.* The difference is subtle but transformative: one closes possibility, the other preserves agency.

Real-world applications are everywhere. Athletes use reframing to recover from mistakes mid-game. A missed shot does not prove incompetence but signals a need to adjust technique. Surgeons employ it under pressure, distinguishing between genuine error and the mind's exaggerations under fatigue. Even in politics, reframing can shift entrenched positions: asking, "What evidence actually supports this belief?" has the power to puncture dogma, though rarely without resistance.

Critics sometimes argue that reframing risks diluting authenticity—that constantly reworking thoughts may lead to denial of genuine emotions. Yet CBT distinguishes between *feeling* and *interpretation*. Fear or sadness is not denied; it is contextualised. The terror of the late-night email is acknowledged, but its catastrophic story is tested. Reframing respects emotion while refusing to let it dictate unquestioned reality.

Philosophically, reframing raises deeper questions. If thoughts are not facts, what is the status of the inner voice? To live without reframing is to be governed by every mental impulse, however distorted. To practise reframing is to admit that much of what we take as "truth" is provisional, shaped by biases and moods. This recognition is unsettling but also liberating: if the mind can deceive, it can also be trained.

The process, however, is not instantaneous. Just as muscles strengthen through repetition, reframing grows through practice. The first attempts may feel artificial—writing down beliefs, weighing them like evidence in a courtroom. Over time, though, the pause between thought and reaction widens. The mind begins to ask automatically: *Is this accurate? What proof do I have? What perspective am I neglecting?* In that pause, a new kind of freedom emerges—the freedom not to be bound by the loudest or darkest thought.

Still, reframing cannot resolve all tension. What about thoughts that reflect real danger, genuine risk, or enduring uncertainty? To reframe in these cases requires nuance: distinguishing between distortion and valid warning. This is where reframing intersects with wisdom—the capacity to know when fear exaggerates, and when it alerts. The question lingers, deliberately unresolved: how do we draw that line with precision, without drifting into denial or paranoia?

Perhaps the task is not to eliminate bias or distortion entirely but to become fluent in recognising their fingerprints. Reframing offers not a perfect filter but a method of inquiry. It keeps the mind honest, tethered to evidence, while still leaving room for intuition and caution. And in a world where information overwhelms, assumptions proliferate, and internal critics shout loudest, such a discipline is not merely therapeutic. It is essential for clarity, resilience, and the possibility of living with greater accuracy and less unnecessary suffering.

The Power of Language

A surgeon preparing for a delicate procedure whispers to herself, *steady hands, focus now.* The words are simple, almost trivial, yet they direct her attention, regulate her breathing, and steady her physiology. In another context, a student facing exams mutters, *I'm going to fail, I always fail.* Here too, the words alter the body: heart rate rises, palms sweat, concentration fractures. In both cases, language does more than describe—it shapes reality from the inside out.

The paradox is stark: words are intangible, yet they wield tangible effects. Internal dialogue is not mere commentary but a driver of emotion and behaviour. Neuroscience confirms this. Studies show that negative self-talk activates the same neural circuits as external criticism, releasing stress hormones and narrowing attentional scope. By contrast, supportive self-talk can enhance performance, modulate stress responses, and even influence pain perception. To speak to oneself is to programme, in part, the operating system of the mind.

Yet this influence is rarely recognised. Most people assume that their inner voice is simply narrating what is true: *I am exhausted, I can't handle this, I'll never be good enough.* They fail to see that these phrases are not objective facts but interpretations—sometimes wildly distorted ones. A more accurate statement might be, *I feel tired right now,* which names a temporary state rather than a permanent identity. The difference is not cosmetic. To say *I am exhausted* fuses the self with fatigue. To say *I feel tired* opens the possibility of rest, recovery, or persistence. Language defines the frame in which action becomes possible.

Psychologists distinguish between *entity language* and *process language*. The first freezes identity—*I am anxious, I am bad at maths, I am lazy*. The second recognises fluidity—*I am experiencing anxiety, I am struggling with this problem, I am finding it difficult to act today*. The former locks the door, the latter leaves it ajar. This shift, subtle yet profound, demonstrates why attention to language matters. Words can imprison or liberate, often without our noticing.

Practical strategies grow from this insight. One technique involves replacing global judgements with specific descriptions. Instead of *I'm a terrible parent,* one might say, *I shouted at my child this morning because I was stressed*. The latter acknowledges a behaviour without collapsing the entire identity into it. Another method draws from cognitive reappraisal: reframing *I must do this perfectly* as *I want to do this well, but mistakes are part of learning*. Again, the change is not platitude but precision—the words redirect expectation from impossible standard to sustainable growth.

Critics warn against the slide into empty affirmations, those hollow mantras of *I am amazing, everything is wonderful,* which collapse under the weight of lived reality. The task is not to replace negativity with saccharine denial but to cultivate accuracy and balance. Evidence-based reframing requires words that ring true, neither catastrophising nor glossing over. A doctor telling herself *I never make mistakes* courts disaster. Telling herself *I am competent and cautious, and I learn from errors* sustains both humility and confidence.

The cultural dimension is equally revealing. Languages encode different ways of experiencing thought. In Japanese, the self is often framed relationally—*watashi wa* situates "I" in context. In many Indigenous languages, verbs dominate over nouns, emphasising process over fixed identity. English, by contrast, privileges the static "I am" construction, which can reinforce self-labelling. This linguistic bias nudges inner dialogue toward permanence: *I am depressed* rather than *I am experiencing depression*. Awareness of this bias allows for intentional correction, a way of loosening language's grip on identity.

Philosophically, the question becomes: do we use words, or do words use us? Wittgenstein argued that the limits of language are the limits of our world. If so, inner dialogue is not just commentary but boundary. By repeating phrases like *I can't cope,* we shrink our world until the statement feels incontrovertible. But if we choose words that reflect possibility—*I don't know how yet, I am learning to cope*—the horizon shifts. Language does not guarantee success, but it preserves the conditions under which success can emerge.

Even small adjustments can have measurable impact. Athletes who reframe nerves as *energy* rather than *fear* often perform better, because the body interprets arousal differently when filtered through language. Students who swap *I have to study* for *I choose to study* report increased motivation; the phrase reminds them of agency rather than obligation. Surgeons who use structured self-instruction (*first incision, check bleeding, proceed slowly*) reduce error rates. In all these cases, language operates not as decoration but as tool.

The challenge is constancy. Under pressure, the mind reverts to familiar grooves. Shifting inner dialogue requires repetition, just as physical training does. Writing down recurring phrases, interrogating their accuracy, and deliberately experimenting with alternatives cultivates a new linguistic reflex. Over time, this reflex reshapes the inner climate—less hostile, more workable, and better aligned with reality.

Still, a question remains unresolved: how far can language carry us? Is there a point where changing words becomes cosmetic, a veneer over deeper suffering? Can shifting *I am broken* to *I am struggling* heal trauma, or is it merely a first step? Here lies the deeper tension: language is powerful but not omnipotent. It can unlock doors, but it cannot by itself rebuild the house. Perhaps its truest value lies not in solving everything but in carving space for other forms of healing to take root.

What is certain is that words matter—not as slogans but as instruments of thought, precision, and possibility. To speak differently to oneself is to live differently. The question is whether we are willing to treat inner language not as background noise but as a force that shapes our emotional and behavioural landscape daily. The answer may determine whether the voice in the head becomes ally or adversary in the pursuit of clarity and resilience.

Practicing Mental Flexibility

A stock market dips, a relationship falters, a deadline looms—and in the space of seconds, the mind can spin into catastrophe. *This is the end. I've ruined everything. I can't handle it.* Yet if the same events are reframed, the spiral softens: *This is difficult, but I've handled challenges before. What's the first step I can take?* The situation is unchanged; the narrative is not. What shifts here is not intelligence or willpower but *mental flexibility*—the ability to loosen rigid patterns of thought and replace panic with perspective.

The paradox is that flexibility, often mistaken for weakness, is in fact a form of strength. Rigid thinking offers a seductive clarity: one answer, one path, one identity. But when reality refuses to cooperate, rigidity fractures. Flexibility, by contrast, bends without breaking. It allows for revision, adjustment, and resilience. In psychology, this capacity is trained through *cognitive restructuring*: the practice of identifying distorted thoughts and reshaping them into balanced, accurate alternatives. Not to delude oneself with false positivity, but to cultivate a mind nimble enough to meet uncertainty without collapse.

Cognitive restructuring lies at the heart of cognitive-behavioural therapy (CBT), one of the most empirically validated approaches in modern psychology. A patient who thinks *I failed this meeting, therefore I'm incompetent* is guided to examine the evidence: *What went wrong? What went right?*

Have I succeeded in other meetings? Through questioning, the thought loosens its grip, and new perspectives surface. Research shows that repeated practice of such reframing reduces symptoms of anxiety and depression, increases problem-solving skills, and fosters greater adaptability under stress. Mental flexibility, in this sense, is not innate temperament but trainable skill.

Consider the elite athlete. A gymnast misses a landing and tells herself, *I'm not good enough for this competition*. If left unchecked, that thought can unravel performance. But with training, she might reframe: *That was one mistake in a routine of twenty skills. My job now is to focus on the next one.* This shift does not deny the error but repositions it. The gymnast preserves confidence and sustains performance. In professional domains as diverse as aviation, surgery, and entrepreneurship, this skill proves decisive: the ability to recover perspective quickly rather than spiral into rigid self-condemnation.

Still, flexibility is not synonymous with constant optimism. It does not mean dismissing pain or pretending setbacks are blessings in disguise. Rather, it means cultivating an inner posture that can hold multiple truths simultaneously: *This is painful* and *this is survivable. I made a mistake* and *I am capable of growth*. In philosophical terms, flexibility resists dualism. It rejects the tyranny of either–or in favour of both–and. Such thinking creates room for nuance, for patience, for the complexity that real life demands.

The mechanics of practicing flexibility often begin with slowing down. Between stimulus and response lies a gap, as Viktor Frankl observed—a space in which choice resides. Cognitive restructuring expands that space. By catching a catastrophic thought—*This project will destroy my career*—and testing it—*What evidence supports this? What evidence contradicts it?*—one generates room for alternative responses. Over time, the reflex to panic is replaced with the reflex to inquire. Inquiry, in turn, opens the possibility of deliberate action.

One striking example comes from military training, where soldiers are taught "stress inoculation." Under simulated high-pressure conditions, they practise reframing automatic catastrophic thoughts into task-focused instructions: *I'm panicking, I can't breathe* becomes *Slow breath, focus on the next step, follow protocol.* Such reframing reduces cortisol levels, preserves working memory, and prevents the kind of tunnel vision that leads to errors in the field. If flexibility can be trained in combat, it can certainly be trained in the office, the classroom, or the home.

Yet the practice requires repetition. Just as muscles strengthen under gradual load, cognitive habits change through consistent application. Writing down distorted thoughts, challenging them with structured questions, and rehearsing alternative perspectives may feel mechanical at first. But with persistence, the practice becomes second nature. Mental flexibility is less a single breakthrough than a discipline—a way of training the mind to return, again and again, to balance.

Still, tension remains. Flexibility has limits. A person cannot endlessly reframe genuine injustice or systemic harm into benign stories without risking denial or self-silencing. At what point does reframing become avoidance? When does perspective become passivity? The challenge, then, is to wield flexibility as a tool of clarity, not as a shield against reality. It should help us see more clearly, not look away.

And perhaps this is the final provocation: in a world where rigidity masquerades as strength, are we willing to practise the subtler courage of bending? Can we train ourselves not only to think differently but to *unthink* when necessary—to discard old certainties, release old scripts, and try on new perspectives until one fits the complexity of the moment? The answers are not tidy, but the willingness to ask such questions may itself be the essence of flexibility.

Chapter 8
The Role of the Body in Quieting the Mind

A boardroom executive once confessed that before every high-stakes presentation, he practised a simple routine: three minutes of deliberate breathing, shoulders back, feet planted firmly on the ground. Without it, he felt hijacked by racing thoughts. With it, he spoke with authority. The paradox is striking—his sharpest tool for calming the mind was not a mental exercise, but a bodily act.

Across cultures and centuries, human beings have turned instinctively to the body in times of mental turbulence: monks pacing cloisters in silent walking meditation, athletes centring themselves through ritual movements, or parents rocking infants in repetitive rhythm. Yet in our modern fixation on mental mastery, we often overlook the body's role in shaping inner quiet. We imagine calmness as an act of will, wrestled into existence by thought alone, when in truth it is often the body that leads and the mind that follows.

This chapter explores the science and practice of that mind–body reciprocity. The nervous system is not a passive backdrop to thought; it is an active player, constantly broadcasting signals of safety or threat. Breath, posture, and movement tune this system up or down, amplifying agitation or inviting stillness. Somatic awareness—learning to feel and inhabit the body—grounds attention in the present, pulling it away from spirals of distraction. Sleep, too, emerges not as a luxury but as the substrate of mental clarity, with its absence fuelling the static of unquiet minds.

Modern neuroscience reveals that this feedback loop is far from metaphorical. The vagus nerve, which connects brain to body, modulates stress and calm with each inhalation and exhalation. Hormones like cortisol rise or fall in rhythm with physical practices. Muscle tension can broadcast alarm signals that perpetuate worry; a relaxed stance can reframe a situation as manageable. Far from being separate realms, body and mind converse continually—and learning their grammar is a discipline as vital as any cognitive training.

What follows will examine how simple practices—progressive relaxation, body scanning, yoga micro-exercises—act as anchors of awareness in hectic lives. We will look at how sleep deprivation magnifies inner chatter, and how deliberate rituals of rest can restore clarity. We will track the ways physical training sharpens attention and why elite performers—from surgeons to musicians—depend on embodied rituals to cultivate mental steadiness.

The larger proposition is radical in its simplicity: calmness is not conjured out of thought but built, piece by piece, from the body upward. This reframing carries practical weight. It suggests that quieting the mind does not always begin with mental effort; sometimes it begins by exhaling slowly, adjusting one's stance, or closing the eyes to rest. If the mind feels ungovernable, the body may be the more faithful doorway.

And so a question arises: if our bodies hold the levers of calm, why do we so often treat them as afterthoughts, tending only to the mind? The answer lies ahead, in the science and practice of turning the body into an ally in the pursuit of inner quiet.

Physiology of Calm

Consider the striking contrast between two ordinary scenes. In the first, a commuter stands on a crowded train, shoulders hunched, jaw clenched, breath shallow and rapid. In the second, a yoga practitioner sits cross-legged, spine lengthened, exhaling in slow, steady waves. The contexts differ, but so too does the biology: in one case the body amplifies stress signals; in the other it sends cues of safety and balance. What is often mistaken as a purely psychological distinction—the presence or absence of calm—is in truth written into the body's posture, rhythm, and movement.

Breathing, posture, and physical activity are not incidental to mental life. They are central regulators of the nervous system, determining whether the body sustains agitation or fosters quiet. For centuries, traditions from Indian pranayama to Greek stoicism have recognised the intimate tie between body and mind, though only recently has neuroscience mapped the circuits that explain why slowing the breath or opening the chest can quiet inner noise. The paradox is that we spend our lives surrounded by techniques for physical calm, but rarely view them as levers of mental clarity.

At the core lies the autonomic nervous system, split broadly into two branches: the sympathetic, which prepares us for action, and the parasympathetic, which restores rest and recovery. Breathing is one of the rare functions that straddles conscious and unconscious control. Rapid, shallow inhalations signal threat, triggering cascades of cortisol and adrenaline. Deep, elongated exhalations, by contrast, stimulate the vagus nerve, shifting physiology towards a parasympathetic state. When people describe "taking a breath to calm down," they are not speaking metaphorically—they are engaging a biological switch.

Posture, too, shapes emotion in ways more profound than many suspect. A collapsed stance, with rounded shoulders and a downward gaze, feeds the nervous system cues of defeat or insecurity. Upright posture, with an open chest and balanced alignment, supports not only musculoskeletal health but also a state of alert yet stable calm. Studies have shown that expansive postures can reduce self-reported stress and even modulate hormonal balances, though such findings are sometimes debated. The broader point stands: how we hold ourselves communicates inward as much as outward.

Movement introduces yet another dimension. Sedentary stillness, when paired with mental tension, often deepens agitation, as muscles tighten without release. Rhythmic movement—walking, stretching, slow repetitive exercise—can discharge accumulated stress and entrain a steadier rhythm of breath and heart rate. This is one reason why anxious minds often find relief in pacing or why contemplative traditions pair prayer with ritual movement. The body seeks motion as a way of metabolising mental unrest.

None of this implies that calmness can be engineered with mechanical precision. There are tensions. Deep breathing may feel intolerable to someone in the grip of panic, and being told to "stand tall" can sound like an empty slogan rather than a practice. Yet the evidence is clear that cultivating bodily awareness opens a channel of influence over mental states. When approached not as rigid technique but as experiment—adjusting breath, shifting posture, introducing movement—the body becomes a laboratory for quieting the mind.

The implications are practical. Before an important conversation, one might pause for three slow breaths to regulate the nervous system. At a desk, noticing and correcting slumped posture can prevent the physical reinforcement of stress. Incorporating short walks or stretches into the day interrupts spirals of tension. These are not lifestyle accessories but interventions that alter the underlying physiology of thought. They make possible the clarity and steadiness that overthinking often obscures.

The larger philosophical lesson is that calmness is not solely a product of rational mastery. It arises from a dialogue between body and mind, a dialogue often neglected in modern accounts of productivity or resilience. To quiet mental noise, one does not always begin by analysing thoughts; one can begin by adjusting the instrument through which those thoughts are sustained—the breathing lungs, the aligned spine, the moving limbs.

And yet, an unresolved question lingers: if such simple practices can so profoundly alter our inner states, why do so many of us resist them, defaulting instead to mental struggle? Perhaps because in attending to the body we admit that control lies not only in intellect but in physiology. To embrace that truth is to broaden our understanding of calm—not as a fragile mood, but as a state rooted in the very fabric of being.

Somatic Awareness

Imagine a person sitting at their desk late into the evening, eyes fixed on a glowing screen. Their mind is racing with deadlines and doubts, yet if they paused to notice, they would feel the jaw clamped, the shoulders lifted towards the ears, the breath trapped high in the chest. The mind screams of overwhelm, but the body whispers the same story in subtler language. Most of us miss it. In our culture of mental overdrive, we are trained to chase solutions in thought, even as the body holds the earliest, clearest signals of strain. Somatic awareness begins with listening to that language again.

To speak of somatic awareness is to speak of a return to presence through the medium of the body. Unlike abstract self-analysis, which often breeds further entanglement, body-based mindfulness is grounded in direct sensation—tightness, warmth, heaviness, or ease. It transforms the body from a silent backdrop into an anchor for attention. This is not new: Buddhist monks practised body scanning centuries ago, and modern psychotherapists have incorporated somatic practices to treat trauma, anxiety, and depression. What neuroscience adds is confirmation: the simple act of tuning into sensation down-regulates the amygdala, dampens stress responses, and recruits networks linked with calm and regulation.

Progressive muscle relaxation offers one of the clearest illustrations. Developed in the early 20th century by physician Edmund Jacobson, it involves systematically tensing and releasing muscle groups. The exercise is deceptively simple—clench the fists, notice the tension, then soften into release. Yet in doing so, the practitioner learns to detect gradations of stress before they escalate. It turns the abstract idea of "relaxing" into something concrete, almost mechanical: a dialogue between contraction and release. Repeated regularly, it rewires one's sensitivity to the earliest signs of tension, offering choice before overwhelm sets in.

Body scanning extends this principle into a more meditative realm. Beginning with the toes and moving steadily upwards, attention is directed to each region in turn, noticing sensations without judgement. One might find warmth in the hands, tightness in the hips, or numbness in the back. The act of noticing is not passive; it interrupts mental chatter by shifting focus from imagined futures to embodied now. Research on mindfulness-based stress reduction (MBSR) programmes consistently finds that body scanning reduces rumination and improves sleep. Its power lies not in fixing sensations but in *staying with them,* learning that discomfort can be observed without immediate reaction.

Micro-practices drawn from yoga add another layer of accessibility. A slow forward fold at the office, a few rounds of cat-cow movement between meetings, or simply pausing to notice the breath in the belly can act as punctuation marks in a frantic day. Unlike longer sessions of meditation, these brief interventions slip easily into modern life. Athletes use them before performance, surgeons between operations, and musicians backstage—not as spiritual rituals, but as nervous-system resets. Each small act reasserts agency over attention.

Of course, somatic awareness is not without resistance. For many, turning attention inward feels alien or uncomfortable, especially if the body holds unprocessed trauma. Sensations can feel threatening precisely because they bypass the filters of rational control. Yet here lies their transformative capacity: by learning to tolerate and observe embodied signals, one builds resilience. What once triggered automatic flight can, over time, become tolerable, even manageable. The body ceases to be a silent saboteur and becomes a guide.

Philosophically, somatic awareness challenges the old Cartesian divide between body and mind. To notice that shallow breathing can intensify worry, or that unclenching the jaw can soften anger, is to dissolve the illusion that thought and flesh are separate. Awareness becomes a loop: the body influences the mind, the mind returns its gaze to the body, and both shift together. Anchoring in sensation does not erase thought; it steadies the field in which thought arises.

The practical implications are profound. A student overwhelmed before an exam might ground themselves by feeling their feet against the floor. A leader preparing for a difficult conversation could scan their body for hidden tension and breathe into it before speaking. A parent caught in the storm of a child's tantrum might unclench their fists and release their shoulders, discovering that calm can begin in muscle before it reaches the mind.

And yet a deeper question persists: if the body holds such reliable gateways to calm, why are we so quick to abandon it in favour of mental noise? Perhaps because thought flatters us with the illusion of control, while sensation asks for vulnerability. To cultivate somatic awareness, then, is not just to practise techniques—it is to accept that clarity begins not in the lofty heights of intellect but in the quiet, humbling ground of the body itself.

Sleep and Cognitive Clarity

There is a cruel irony at work in modern life: the very state we sacrifice in order to be more productive is the one most essential to productivity. Sleep, treated by many as a negotiable luxury, is in fact the brain's foundational mode of maintenance. When deprived of it, we do not merely grow tired—we lose clarity, resilience, and coherence of thought. Insufficient rest does not only blur the edges of cognition; it amplifies the noise within, fuelling the very mental chatter we hope to silence by pushing through.

Consider the findings of the Walker Sleep Lab at the University of California, which show that even a single night of restricted sleep heightens amygdala reactivity by nearly 60 per cent. In practical terms, this means that without rest, the brain becomes emotionally volatile, over-interpreting minor stressors as threats. The result is a mind primed for catastrophic thinking and self-critical spirals. Poor sleep does not just dull the intellect—it turns up the volume on inner noise, making worries louder and harder to regulate.

Neuroscience has revealed why. Sleep is not passive downtime but an active process of housekeeping. During deep slow-wave sleep, the glymphatic system flushes metabolic waste, including beta-amyloid proteins implicated in neurodegeneration. REM sleep, by contrast, integrates emotional experiences, stripping them of their sharpest sting while preserving their lessons. When either stage is cut short, the mind carries the residue of unprocessed stress into waking life. Rumination becomes sticky, memory less reliable, and attention frays at the edges. What feels like "overthinking" is often the brain struggling to compensate for unfinished overnight work.

Modern examples abound. Surgeons deprived of rest after night shifts commit errors at rates comparable to alcohol intoxication. Pilots, athletes, and even financial traders—all professions where focus is paramount—show precipitous declines in performance when sleep is curtailed. For the average professional, the effects may not involve life-or-death stakes, but they manifest in quieter forms: the inability to concentrate during meetings, the re-reading of the same paragraph without comprehension, the late-night spiral of replaying conversations with distorted intensity.

Yet cultural narratives continue to glorify sleeplessness. The "I'll sleep when I'm dead" ethos persists in entrepreneurial circles, as though endurance were synonymous with excellence. Philosophically, this reveals a deep mistrust of stillness. We equate rest with laziness, forgetting that the capacity for deliberate thought requires an alternation between activity and recovery. Just as muscles grow stronger in the intervals between training, so too does cognition refine itself during periods of deep sleep.

If rest is essential, how then do we reclaim it in an age of relentless stimulation? Research points to the efficacy of simple rituals. A consistent sleep schedule anchors circadian rhythms, while dimming lights in the evening signals the pineal gland to release melatonin. Avoiding screens before bed reduces blue-light interference, but more subtly, it creates a psychological boundary between the busyness of the day and the descent into rest. For many, presleep routines such as gentle stretching, mindful breathing, or journalling to externalise worries serve as cues that the mind can safely release its grip.

More innovative interventions have emerged too. Cognitive behavioural therapy for insomnia (CBT-I) teaches individuals to challenge catastrophic sleep beliefs ("If I don't sleep eight hours, tomorrow will be ruined") and to associate the bed strictly with sleep, not with work or scrolling. Studies consistently show CBT-I to outperform sleeping pills in the long run, restoring not just hours of rest but a healthier relationship to it. Even brief relaxation techniques—progressive muscle release or slow diaphragmatic breathing—can reduce sleep latency, quieting both body and mind.

But there remains a tension worth acknowledging. Sleep cannot be forced; it must be invited. The paradox is that the more we obsess over securing it, the more elusive it becomes. This raises a deeper point: perhaps cultivating restorative rest is less about engineering control and more about surrendering to rhythm. Ancient traditions understood this intuitively, framing sleep as a daily practice of letting go, a rehearsal for mortality itself.

In this light, the question becomes not simply *how do we sleep more?* but *how do we relearn to trust sleep as a natural ally?* For until we do, we will continue to fight the mind's static with more thought, overlooking the quieter truth: that clarity is not only found in the discipline of wakefulness but in the humility of rest.

The Mind-Body Feedback Loop

A curious thing happens when you stand tall, straighten your back, and slow your breathing: your mind changes. The storm of thoughts that seemed unmanageable just moments before begins to soften, and perspective re-emerges. This is not imagination. It is physiology speaking to psychology—an ancient dialogue often ignored in the modern fixation on treating the mind as an isolated command centre.

Take the example of heart rate variability (HRV), a measure of the time between heartbeats. Elite athletes monitor it closely because it reflects the body's adaptability under stress. Higher HRV correlates with resilience, calm, and focus; lower HRV, with anxiety and depletion. What is striking is that HRV can be consciously influenced through slow, paced breathing. In other words, by altering breath, you change cardiovascular rhythms, which in turn send signals back to the brain, recalibrating emotional state. Calmness here is not a vague aspiration but a trainable, embodied skill.

This feedback loop extends far beyond breath. Posture has measurable effects on mental states. Studies in embodied cognition show that slumping not only communicates defeat to others but reinforces it internally, increasing feelings of helplessness. Conversely, adopting upright, expansive positions activates neuroendocrine pathways that reduce cortisol and increase testosterone, subtly shifting one's sense of agency. Behavioural experiments confirm what military training and performing arts have long intuited: the way we hold the body can script the mind's response to challenge.

Movement is another profound lever. Aerobic exercise releases endorphins and elevates serotonin, buffering against depression, while resistance training sharpens cognitive control through upregulation of brain-derived neurotrophic factor (BDNF), a molecule essential for neuroplasticity. Even brief bouts of physical activity alter neural chemistry in ways no amount of abstract reasoning can replicate. The philosopher who spends twelve hours at a desk may outthink herself into paralysis, while the one who walks daily finds fresh clarity mid-stride.

Sceptics might counter that such links oversimplify—that posture, breath, or exercise cannot "cure" existential dread or complex trauma. And they are correct: no single bodily adjustment resolves life's deeper struggles. But what these practices *do* is create the conditions in which clarity is possible. They shift baseline physiology from threat to safety, allowing higher cognitive functions to engage. Without this reset, strategies for reframing thoughts or making choices remain fragile, undermined by a nervous system locked in survival mode.

Consider how yoga is used in trauma therapy. Not as a spiritual add-on but as a direct intervention to regulate the autonomic nervous system. Survivors learn to notice sensations, re-establish boundaries of control, and anchor in the present through embodied practice. The act of stretching or focusing on a muscle is not trivial—it is a signal to the nervous system that it can stand down. Calmness emerges not from suppression but from re-patterning the feedback between body and mind.

This raises a philosophical tension: if our mental states are so influenced by physiology, where does agency truly lie?

Are we puppets of biology, tricked into tranquillity by posture and breath? Or does recognising this loop expand our agency, offering us more tools to participate consciously in our own regulation? The latter seems the richer interpretation. To attend to the body is not to reduce the self but to enlarge it, weaving mind and body into a dynamic partnership rather than an adversarial divide.

Modern workplaces often illustrate the neglect of this principle. Endless hours at screens, collapsed posture, shallow breathing—all conspire to amplify noise, yet interventions are sought solely through mental frameworks: productivity hacks, resilience seminars, cognitive reframing. Rarely is the loop closed with body-first practices. Yet when leaders incorporate short movement breaks, encourage mindful breathing before meetings, or simply design spaces that allow upright sitting and walking, the change in collective tone is unmistakable.

Perhaps the most radical implication is that calmness itself should be reframed. It is not a passive absence of agitation nor a trait some are born with. It is a skill, cultivated through the ongoing dialogue of breath, movement, and posture feeding back into the brain's regulatory circuits. What appears as psychological resilience is often embodied literacy—the ability to work with the body to shape the mind.

The deeper question, then, is not whether the loop exists—it does—but how far we are willing to take responsibility for it. If calmness is built from the body upward, are we prepared to reimagine our daily practices, our workplaces, even our cultural attitudes, around this truth? The answer is not yet clear, but what is undeniable is that the path to clarity may begin with something as simple, and as radical, as the next breath.

Chapter 9
The Noise of Others

In a crowded café, a woman lifts her phone for the tenth time in as many minutes. Notifications flash: a colleague's email, a friend's holiday photos, a news alert about an unfolding crisis. Her coffee cools as her mind fractures—one thought pulled to work deadlines, another to envy at a sun-drenched beach, a third to fear of global uncertainty. By the time she looks up, the world around her feels louder than before. This is not an exceptional moment but an ordinary one, repeated in countless variations across modern life.

We often imagine noise as external—traffic, chatter, construction. Yet some of the most exhausting noise we carry is imported through others: the comparisons sparked by social media feeds, the subtle weight of expectation from peers, the silent demand to be available, responsive, curated. The paradox is stark: we live in the most connected age in human history, and yet never has the mind had to process so many competing signals from other people's lives. The consequence is a constant murmur of evaluation, replay, and anticipation—mental static not generated by us alone, but triggered by the presence and pressure of others.

The anthropologist Robin Dunbar proposed that human cognition evolved to manage a social group of around 150 people. Today, even the least active social media user may be passively keeping up with hundreds or thousands. Add to that the relentless presence of colleagues, family obligations, digital communities, and cultural norms, and we find ourselves inhabiting a bandwidth far beyond what evolution prepared us for. The mind strains to keep pace, filling the gaps with speculation: *What do they think of me? Am I keeping up? Did I say the wrong thing?* It is no wonder that silence, when it arrives, feels alien.

This chapter examines the ways others amplify or quiet our inner noise. It begins with the phenomenon of *social overload*—how constant communication, comparison, and exposure to curated lives push our minds into a perpetual state of self-monitoring. From there, we turn to the *performance trap,* the cultural expectation to present a polished version of ourselves, and how that pressure reshapes our internal dialogue into one of inadequacy and striving. Yet it is not all burden: relationships, at their best, can provide grounding. We will explore how certain bonds—whether with friends, family, or mentors—help quieten the static, while others magnify it. Finally, we consider the act of redrawing boundaries: how digital hygiene, intentional solitude, and conscious reconnection can create an environment in which attention, clarity, and presence have a chance to flourish.

The stakes are not trivial. To neglect the role of others in our mental life is to miss one of the most potent sources of noise and, paradoxically, of quiet. The challenge lies in discerning which connections elevate us and which entangle us; which demands are genuine responsibilities and which are self-imposed performances. The answer is rarely simple, for humans are both social and solitary creatures, craving belonging while guarding autonomy.

What if learning to quiet the mind is not only an inward task but a social one? What if the path to clarity requires us not just to manage thoughts but to reshape the ecology of relationships, cultures, and digital environments in which those thoughts are triggered? These questions open the door to the chapters that follow, urging us to reconsider not only how we think, but with whom—and in what company—we choose to think at all.

Social Overload

At dawn in Tokyo, a young office worker wakes to the vibration of her phone. Before she has even left her futon, she has skimmed overnight emails, glanced at global markets, responded to a friend's late-night message, and scrolled through a dozen updates on Instagram. Her first thoughts of the day are not her own but borrowed—snippets of other people's moods, achievements, fears, and demands. She has yet to speak a word aloud, yet she is already saturated. This is not an unusual morning, nor unique to Japan. It is a morning replicated, in slightly altered form, across the globe.

The paradox of our time is that we have never been more connected and never more internally scattered. Where earlier generations began their day in relative quiet—newspapers, neighbours, perhaps a radio broadcast—today's mind is bombarded from the moment of waking. The consequence is subtle but corrosive: an interior landscape shaped not by the slow rhythm of one's own thoughts but by the constant influx of external stimuli. Mental chatter multiplies, echoing the clamour of others.

To understand this phenomenon, psychologists have begun to describe what might be called *social overload*: the cognitive and emotional strain produced by unrelenting interaction, exposure, and comparison. Human cognition evolved in small, tightly knit groups where social bonds were vital for survival. The brain is exquisitely attuned to monitoring others' status, intentions, and opinions. But the architecture that once allowed us to track the moods of a few dozen kin now attempts to process the curated lives of thousands. Each notification cues vigilance: *Am I keeping up? Did I respond in time? Why wasn't I included?* What was once an adaptive sensitivity now becomes a source of static.

The role of comparison is particularly insidious. Social media platforms function as amplifiers of envy and insecurity, offering endless opportunities to measure one's life against carefully edited glimpses of others. The philosopher Søren Kierkegaard once warned that comparison is the thief of joy, but our technologies have industrialised the process. Even when we consciously know that an image is staged or filtered, the emotional impact remains. The result is not merely a passing pang of envy but a persistent undercurrent of self-evaluation: a background hum of inadequacy that shapes the very texture of thought.

Nor is the problem limited to social media. Workplaces, too, contribute to overload, with their perpetual messaging platforms and expectation of real-time responsiveness. The old distinction between work and rest has collapsed into an "always on" rhythm, in which the mind is required to process social signals—tone of an email, timing of a reply, subtle shifts in managerial language—at all hours. Even leisure has been colonised by social vigilance: the need to post, to comment, to maintain visibility. In this sense, the modern individual is never fully off-stage.

Yet it would be simplistic to argue that social connectivity is purely corrosive. Humans are profoundly relational beings, and isolation can generate its own form of noise—rumination untempered by external perspective, loneliness that distorts self-appraisal. The challenge lies in balance: discerning when connection nourishes and when it overwhelms. Studies on "social buffering" show that supportive interactions can mitigate stress responses, lowering cortisol and reducing perceived threat. But the same pathways that allow connection to soothe us are those that, when over-stimulated, flood the mind with noise.

Consider the case of a teenager navigating friendships online. Affirmation—likes, comments, messages—triggers dopamine release, reinforcing the behaviour. But the absence of response, or the perception of exclusion, activates the same neural circuitry associated with physical pain. The mind is wired to treat social signals as vital, and in a sense they are. Yet when multiplied to excess, the very circuits designed to keep us attuned become hijacked. The chatter that follows—*Did I do something wrong? Should I change?*—is not incidental but the predictable consequence of an overloaded social brain.

Philosophically, this raises an unsettling question: how much of what we consider our *own* thoughts are in fact echoes of others? When our attention is colonised by the demands and projections of hundreds of voices, the line between inner and outer blurs. The "noise of others" becomes indistinguishable from the noise of the self, until we mistake second-hand concerns for personal truths. To reclaim clarity, one must first recognise this porousness: that the mind is not a sealed chamber but a resonant chamber, vibrating with the frequencies of its environment.

And yet, what would it mean to redraw those boundaries in practice? To decide, deliberately, which voices enter, and which are turned down? The very notion is countercultural in a world that equates connectivity with relevance, responsiveness with value. But without such discernment, the risk is clear: to live a life whose inner soundtrack is dictated less by authentic thought than by the relentless echoes of others.

The unresolved tension remains: we cannot, nor should we, withdraw from society entirely. To be human is to be in relation. The question, then, is not whether we allow others into our mental space, but on what terms. How can we create conditions where connection enriches rather than depletes, where interaction sharpens rather than scatters, where the mind, exposed to the voices of others, does not lose its own?

The Performance Trap

On a quiet Sunday morning in New York, a young professional takes a photograph of her coffee beside a neatly arranged notebook. The table is cleared, the light angled just so, the caption rehearsed in her head before she presses publish. Within minutes, the likes arrive. Yet even as they accumulate, a whisper of doubt grows louder: *Was it authentic enough? Did it measure up?* What began as a private ritual of stillness becomes another stage for judgement. The moment of living has been converted into a performance, and the mind—ever watchful of audience reaction—becomes its harshest critic.

The paradox is striking. Never before has society insisted more on "authenticity," yet never have individuals been more compelled to curate, polish, and project themselves. From job interviews to Instagram feeds, from academic CVs to dating profiles, life is increasingly mediated by an invisible crowd, real or imagined. We become both actors and spectators, constructing narratives about who we are while simultaneously doubting the adequacy of our roles. Beneath the polish lies a chronic unease: the suspicion that the self on display is never quite enough.

This is the essence of the performance trap: the compulsion to live as if perpetually on stage, managing impressions, scripting identities, and filtering reality. It is not confined to celebrities or influencers; it permeates classrooms, boardrooms, and family gatherings alike. Students learn to frame their achievements for admissions committees. Employees cultivate personal brands to remain competitive in fluid labour markets. Even friendships are shaped by strategic disclosures, carefully balancing vulnerability with presentability. The result is an internal dialogue shaped less by genuine reflection than by rehearsals of how one will appear.

Psychologists point to a mechanism known as *self-presentation theory*: the human tendency to control how others perceive us. In moderation, it is adaptive—helping us navigate social groups and maintain cohesion. But in contemporary culture, where platforms magnify visibility and metrics quantify approval, the impulse mutates into an exhausting vigilance. The self is no longer lived but monitored, revised, and endlessly compared against imagined standards. What begins as performance for others becomes performance for oneself, generating an inner loop of critique: *Could I have said it better? Should I have looked different? Why do they seem more successful, more polished, more at ease?*

The damage is not merely psychological but existential. When life is filtered through the lens of performance, moments lose their intrinsic weight. A walk in the park is evaluated for its photographability; a career achievement is judged by how it plays on LinkedIn. The very categories of worth—success, beauty, intelligence, even kindness—become externalised, measured not by lived meaning but by audience reception. The trap is subtle yet suffocating: we begin to experience our lives as spectators rather than participants, alienated from the raw immediacy of being.

There is, however, a tension worth recognising. Performance is not entirely false. Sociologist Erving Goffman argued decades ago that all social life is theatrical: we wear roles, manage impressions, adapt to context. To eliminate performance altogether would be neither possible nor desirable. The problem arises when the performance ceases to serve the living person and instead dictates it. When the need to maintain an image overwhelms the capacity to inhabit one's life, the role devours the actor.

Consider the modern workplace. Professionals are encouraged to "bring their whole selves to work," yet they are simultaneously appraised against rigid metrics of productivity, efficiency, and cultural fit. The contradiction fosters a relentless internal chatter: *Am I being genuine, or am I performing? If I am performing, is that inherently dishonest—*

or simply survival? In such environments, the line between authentic expression and strategic self-fashioning blurs to the point of invisibility.

The same applies in personal domains. Parents curate images of family life that mask exhaustion and conflict. Couples stage happiness for the gaze of friends. Individuals, in pursuit of "authentic branding," rehearse vulnerability until it, too, becomes another product. The inner voice, exposed to these contradictions, grows harsher: *If others seem able to maintain their image, why do I struggle?* The narrative of inadequacy takes root, fuelled by the illusion that others' performances are their realities.

Philosophically, the performance trap reveals a deeper human anxiety: the fear that one's unadorned self may not be enough. The cultural machinery of likes, followers, ratings, and metrics exploits this anxiety, offering temporary reassurance at the cost of long-term erosion of self-trust. The more one seeks validation through performance, the less one learns to rest in unperformed being. Silence becomes intolerable because it provides no applause.

And yet, the question lingers: what would life feel like if we loosened the grip of performance, if moments were lived for themselves rather than their audience value? To step out of the performance trap is not to abandon social roles but to reorient them—to remember that the worth of a life cannot be fully staged, curated, or quantified.

The paradox remains unresolved: we are social beings, inevitably seen and judged. But must we also be perpetually performing? Or might there be a way to stand, even briefly, off-stage—to reclaim the raw immediacy of experience, and to trust that a life lived authentically, though messier and less polished, may ultimately be more sufficient than any performance could ever be?

The Role of Relationships

On any given evening, two people might return home from work with nearly identical burdens of fatigue and uncertainty. One is greeted with warmth: a partner listens without judgement, a child's laughter breaks the day's residue, a friend's text affirms solidarity. The noise in their head, once buzzing, softens. The other arrives to criticism, dismissal, or silence. Their worries, instead of easing, multiply. The same human nervous system that can be lulled into calm by a compassionate presence can be inflamed into chaos by dissonant relationships.

It is a paradox as old as civilisation: the people who sustain us can just as readily unsettle us. Relationships function not as neutral background but as amplifiers—sometimes muting mental static, sometimes dialling it to intolerable levels. Neuroscientific studies reinforce what poets and philosophers have long intuited: our minds are not solitary chambers but open systems, continuously regulated by the signals of those around us. A reassuring glance can quiet cortisol spikes; a hostile remark can set the amygdala ablaze. To speak of inner noise without reference to others is to overlook one of its primary engines.

The family is often the first theatre where this becomes visible. A child raised in an environment of consistent attunement—where caregivers respond with empathy rather than scorn—develops a baseline of internal quiet.

Their inner voice, modelled on external voices, becomes a guide rather than a persecutor. Conversely, environments of criticism or neglect seed self-talk that mimics those early tones. Long into adulthood, the mind replays parental cadences: *You're not good enough. Don't make mistakes. Why can't you do better?* Thus, mental noise often bears the accent of our earliest relationships.

In professional life, the same dynamics surface in subtler but equally potent ways. A manager who offers clarity and support can reduce cognitive load, freeing an employee's attention for creativity. A colleague who undermines or competes triggers vigilance and defensive rumination. Research on "toxic workplaces" repeatedly shows that the psychological cost of poor relationships often outweighs even the demands of the job itself. It is not only *what* we do that shapes the chatter of our minds, but *with whom* we do it.

Friendships, too, play a decisive role. The quiet confidence fostered by a circle of supportive peers can buffer the storms of self-doubt. Yet social comparison—especially when amplified by digital platforms—turns even friendships into sources of mental noise. The paradox intensifies: the same friend whose presence brings joy can also provoke insecurity when their curated successes highlight our perceived shortcomings. Relationships are never static; they oscillate between soothing and stirring our inner soundscape.

Philosophically, this raises an essential question: where does the self end and the other begin? If my calm is contingent on another's tone, is my mind truly my own? Some traditions emphasise radical self-sufficiency, warning against dependence on the affirmation of others. Yet neuroscience suggests an interdependence too profound to ignore. The human nervous system is designed for co-regulation; oxytocin, mirror neurons, and vagal pathways make us porous to each other. Perhaps the challenge is not to sever the influence of others but to discern which relationships foster clarity and which perpetuate static.

This discernment requires courage. It is easier to stay enmeshed in noisy connections than to redraw boundaries. But the act of curating relationships—choosing which voices are granted access to our inner stage—is central to mental health. It does not demand isolation but intentionality. Seeking environments of respect and trust, limiting exposure to corrosive dynamics, and nurturing ties that allow for silence as much as speech—all these shape the texture of inner life.

The irony is that while relationships are a major source of mental noise, they also hold the most powerful antidote. Solitude can provide respite, but lasting quiet often emerges in connection: in dialogue where one is fully heard, in companionship that requires no performance, in love that offers not a mirror of inadequacy but a sanctuary of acceptance. To navigate the role of relationships, then, is to accept their double-edged nature: the same ties that can bind us in noise can also free us into stillness.

The tension remains unresolved. We cannot live without others, yet we cannot grant every voice unfiltered access to the corridors of our mind. The essential task is not to escape relationship but to refine it—to choose deliberately, to listen selectively, and to recognise that the architecture of our inner world is built as much by the presence of others as by the solitude of our own thought. And so the pressing question emerges: how might we learn to let the right voices in while quieting those that echo too loudly within?

Redrawing Boundaries

Consider the quiet revolution of the "Do Not Disturb" function on a phone. A simple crescent moon icon, tapped once, silences the endless buzz of messages, alerts, and pings. To some it is a minor convenience; to others, a radical act of self-preservation. The gesture symbolises something much larger than digital etiquette: the deliberate reclaiming of psychic space from a world that encroaches without pause. In an age where attention is harvested as commodity and availability is worn as virtue, boundaries are no longer optional—they are lifelines.

The paradox of modern connectedness is stark. Never before have humans been so reachable, yet never before has solitude felt so endangered. The same networks that promise belonging often deliver exhaustion. Group chats proliferate, emails multiply, social feeds scroll infinitely, each demanding a sliver of cognitive energy. What is framed as *connection* often operates as a colonisation of inner quiet. The price of constant contact is not merely time lost but mental clarity eroded. Boundaries, then, are not walls of withdrawal but structures of survival.

The notion of boundaries has always existed, of course, though historically they were imposed by circumstance. Nightfall once guaranteed a pause in correspondence; physical distance enforced reprieve from intrusion. Today, technology has dismantled those natural buffers, leaving individuals responsible for erecting their own. Digital hygiene is one such practice: intentional curation of what enters the mental field. It might mean scheduled screen-free hours, pruning notification settings, or even rethinking one's social media diet. Just as food shapes the body, digital intake shapes the mind. Without discipline, the chatter of others bleeds seamlessly into one's own inner monologue.

Intentional solitude is the second boundary often neglected. Solitude is not synonymous with loneliness; it is the fertile soil from which insight and resilience grow. Writers, scientists, and spiritual leaders alike have long emphasised the necessity of deliberate retreat. Blaise Pascal once observed that humanity's troubles stem from our inability to sit quietly in a room alone. Neuroscience now supports the claim: moments of undistracted solitude foster default-mode processing, where the brain integrates experience, incubates creativity, and restores attentional resources. To redraw boundaries is to recognise solitude not as luxury but as daily sustenance.

Yet boundaries must not become rigid fortresses. Human beings require connection, and healthy connection can itself be a boundary against mental noise. The distinction lies in quality rather than quantity. Relationships rooted in respect, presence, and reciprocity provide signals of safety that quiet the nervous system. By contrast, performative or extractive ties amplify the static of inadequacy and vigilance. Redrawing boundaries, therefore, includes auditing not only digital input but relational environments—choosing where openness nourishes and where withdrawal protects.

Still, the practice is fraught with tension. To set boundaries risks disappointing others, inviting accusations of detachment or arrogance. Cultures that prize constant responsiveness may frame refusal as antisocial. But boundaries are not rejections of others; they are affirmations of clarity. They signal that one's mental space is not an open commons but a garden requiring tending. The philosopher Epictetus counselled that freedom begins when one learns to distinguish between what is within one's control and what is not. Boundaries enact that wisdom in the social sphere: I cannot control the flood of external demands, but I can decide which to admit into the sanctum of attention.

The question, then, becomes one of design. How might an individual construct boundaries that are firm enough to preserve clarity yet flexible enough to sustain meaningful connection? There is no single blueprint. For some, it might mean rituals of digital Sabbath, a day unplugged. For others, it may involve micro-practices—closing the laptop at a fixed hour, reserving the first moments of morning for silence rather than scrolling. Each choice represents a rebalancing: noise reduced, clarity reclaimed.

The larger implication is profound. Boundaries are not merely defensive but creative. By limiting intrusion, they carve the space in which thought deepens, relationships mature, and presence intensifies. Without them, life becomes a reactive cascade of stimuli. With them, life regains rhythm. And yet the challenge endures: in a culture that equates constant connection with relevance, how far can one retreat without risking exclusion? At what point does boundary-setting transform from self-care into withdrawal from the shared world? These questions remain open, inviting each reader to experiment, recalibrate, and discover where their own lines must be drawn.

Chapter 10
Finding Constructive Silence

In the winter of 2010, a group of neuroscientists ran a peculiar experiment. Mice were exposed to different sounds—white noise, ambient music, even the sound of other mice. Yet what reshaped their brains most profoundly was not sound at all but its absence. Two hours of daily silence led to the growth of new cells in the hippocampus, the region critical for memory and learning. Silence, it seemed, was not a void but a catalyst. The finding echoed something monks, poets, and philosophers had intuited for centuries: quiet is not merely the absence of noise but a presence of its own, a fertile state that resets both body and mind.

Silence has always unnerved societies obsessed with progress. To pause feels, at first glance, like wasted potential. Yet the very act of pausing—whether in a sentence, a day, or a life—often reveals more than relentless motion. Consider the monastic cloisters of medieval Europe, where silence was both spiritual discipline and social architecture. In the spaces between words, monks claimed, truth could emerge unclouded by the ego's chatter. Fast forward to the present: modern neuroscience now affirms what those ascetics sensed. Brief intervals of silence reduce cortisol, regulate heart rhythms, and restore attentional control, operating as a neurological reset in a world addicted to stimulus.

The question is not whether silence matters but how to reclaim it in lives engineered for interruption. Constructive silence is different from the silence of suppression, avoidance, or alienation. It is not an absence imposed by circumstance but a practice chosen with intent. The person who steps away from their phone for ten minutes, sits in a quiet corner, or simply lets a conversation breathe is not withdrawing but recalibrating. They are making space for clarity to surface where noise once reigned.

Silence also carries symbolic weight beyond the individual. In conversation, it signals respect. To pause after someone speaks is to grant their words full gravity, to resist the reflex of rebuttal or self-display. Skilled negotiators, seasoned therapists, and empathetic friends alike know the value of letting silence do the heavy lifting. In these moments, it becomes less an emptiness than a shared vessel—an interval where understanding takes root. This social silence stands in radical contrast to the barrage of digital interactions, where immediacy often trumps depth and where thoughtful pauses are replaced with compulsive responses.

Equally countercultural is the practice of doing nothing. In societies that fetishise productivity, idleness is mistaken for failure. Yet research shows that periods of rest activate the brain's default mode network, a system linked to creativity, memory consolidation, and emotional regulation. Many of humanity's breakthroughs—from Einstein's thought experiments to Virginia Woolf's literary insights—were conceived not in busyness but in apparent idleness. To rediscover the value of unoccupied time is to rebel against a culture that equates worth with output, reminding ourselves that silence and stillness are not detours from life but conditions for perceiving it more fully.

This chapter will examine silence as discipline, sanctuary, provocation, and signal. It will consider how to create micro-environments for quiet, whether in the solitude of a chair turned toward a window or in a household that chooses an hour free from devices. It will look at silence's role in relationships, where it can deepen trust, and in the inner life, where it can reveal unacknowledged truths. Most of all, it will propose silence not as escape but as resource—a practice that strengthens clarity in a culture increasingly defined by noise.

Yet even as we turn toward silence, tension lingers. How much quiet is nourishing, and when does it tip into isolation? How can silence serve as tool for presence without becoming an excuse for withdrawal? These are questions without simple answers, and it is precisely in the space they open that silence proves its worth. For silence, unlike speech, does not rush to fill gaps with certainty. It leaves room for possibility.

The Discipline of Pausing

In 1968, amidst the clamour of political unrest and cultural upheaval, Thomas Merton, the Trappist monk and writer, collapsed in Bangkok and died suddenly at the age of fifty-three. His life had been marked by words—sermons, journals, essays—but it was the silence of his monastic vocation that shaped him most profoundly. Merton believed that silence was not the absence of life but its intensification. To pause, to retreat from the endless stream of speech and noise, was to find a clarity inaccessible in any other way. His insight resonates today in a world far louder and more distracted than the one he left behind. What he called the discipline of silence, we might now understand as the discipline of pausing.

The paradox of pausing is that it feels counterintuitive in the very moments when it is most needed. The high-pressure executive who reacts instantly to a confrontational email, the parent who snaps at a child in frustration, the citizen scrolling endlessly through digital feeds—all would benefit from a pause, yet the momentum of modern life urges speed. Neuroscience now provides the mechanism behind this paradox. Our brains are wired for rapid response: the amygdala fires, cortisol surges, and action follows before reflection has time to intervene. The pause is not natural; it must be trained. But once cultivated, it creates space between stimulus and response—a space in which perspective, choice, and wisdom can breathe.

Historically, silence has been treated not as deprivation but as discipline. The monastic traditions of Christianity, Buddhism, and Sufism each developed practices of deliberate quiet: vigils, retreats, periods of vow-bound silence. These pauses were not intended to mute the individual but to amplify awareness. In the desert cells of the early Christian monks, silence was regarded as the crucible in which inner noise could be burned away. Zen masters taught that stillness between breaths revealed truths inaccessible to the discursive mind. The Islamic mystics, the Sufis, regarded silence as a kind of fasting for the soul, a way of abstaining from verbal clutter to sharpen one's sense of the divine. Across cultures, the pause was never mere absence but a deliberate act of orientation, a resetting of attention toward what mattered most.

Modern science echoes these ancient intuitions. Studies show that even brief periods of silence—two minutes of stillness after listening to music, for instance—produce greater relaxation and sharper cognitive recovery than exposure to soothing sounds alone. The nervous system shifts into parasympathetic dominance: heart rate slows, blood pressure eases, and stress hormones diminish. Silence, paradoxically, speaks directly to the body. It is a physiological reset, a recalibration of the entire system that undergirds attention, mood, and resilience. The pause is not ornamental; it is biological necessity.

Yet silence today is harder to access than ever. Our environments conspire against it: offices hum with background chatter, streets throb with engines, and homes are infiltrated by the endless pings of digital alerts. True silence is rare. But the discipline of pausing does not require absolute quiet. It requires intention. A person may pause in the midst of traffic by focusing on the rhythm of breath. They may pause in the office by letting a moment of stillness settle before replying to a colleague. They may pause at home by choosing to let a conversation breathe rather than filling every gap with words. In each case, the pause interrupts automaticity and creates an aperture through which awareness can expand.

There is also a social dimension to the pause. In conversation, silence often feels uncomfortable, something to be rushed through or filled. But skilled communicators know that silence can deepen connection. Therapists use pauses to allow clients to process emotion. Orators deploy pauses to give weight to their words, letting meaning resonate. Friends and lovers who can share silence without anxiety often exhibit the strongest bonds. To pause in dialogue is to resist the compulsion of self-display and instead cultivate receptivity. In this way, silence becomes not withdrawal but generosity.

The discipline of pausing, then, is less about disengagement than about re-engagement on different terms. It trains the mind to step back from compulsive reaction, the body to downshift from chronic arousal, and relationships to open space for genuine presence. But this discipline is fragile, constantly under siege by the momentum of modern life. It requires cultivation—daily rituals, intentional practices, and a reframing of silence from void to resource.

And yet, even as silence heals, it provokes questions. Can the pause ever become avoidance, a retreat from responsibility rather than a preparation for it? Might silence be misused, not as reset but as weapon or withdrawal? These tensions remain unresolved. But perhaps that is the point: the value of the pause lies not in definitive answers but in the space it creates for new possibilities to emerge. Silence does not close the conversation. It keeps it open.

Creating Sacred Spaces

On the outskirts of Kyoto, there is a small Zen temple where the monks maintain a rock garden raked into meticulous patterns each morning. The garden contains no flowers, no water, no ornament—just gravel, rocks, and lines. To the uninitiated, it appears barren. Yet for centuries, visitors have described it as one of the most calming places on earth. The arrangement is deliberate: a space emptied of distraction, designed to still the mind and invite attention inward. What matters is not the objects themselves but the atmosphere they create.

Most of us will never rake gravel at dawn in a monastery, yet the principle of such spaces is transferable. Sacredness, in this context, does not necessarily denote religious devotion. It denotes intentionality. A chair in a quiet corner, a candle lit at dusk, the daily ritual of stepping outside before work to breathe the morning air—each can be transformed into a sanctuary if approached with deliberate design. The sacred is not found in grand architecture alone but in the quiet signalling of a place or act that says: *this is where the noise recedes.*

The modern world, however, resists such sanctuaries. Homes are crowded with devices, workplaces hum with perpetual connectivity, and even leisure is colonised by screens. The result is a fragmentation of attention, a constant leakage of inner resources into the demands of the external. To counter this, one must design environments that hold the line. Neuroscience shows that physical surroundings shape mental states: clutter elevates cortisol, while ordered environments reduce cognitive load. Just as athletes prepare arenas for performance and musicians tune their instruments before playing, so too can we prepare micro-environments that prime the mind for clarity.

These spaces need not be large, but they must be intentional. A chair set aside only for reading or reflection acquires symbolic weight: when you sit there, your body learns to associate it with focus and calm. A corner desk cleared of all but essential tools becomes a zone where work is undertaken with depth rather than distraction. Even a few minutes of candlelight at the end of the day can cue the nervous system to downshift from vigilance to rest. The key is consistency—ritualised repetition that trains the body and brain to respond to environmental signals with the desired state of mind.

Consider the strategies of performers at the highest levels. Concert pianists often have pre-performance rituals involving a specific stool, a particular sequence of stretches, even a lucky object placed nearby. Neurosurgeons speak of "sterile focus," cultivated not just by surgical scrubbing but by the choreography of their operating theatre. These examples are extreme, but they illuminate a universal truth: environments condition us. If we wish to reclaim quiet, we must train ourselves not only through mental practice but through the shaping of space.

At the same time, creating sacred spaces is not solely about isolation. The paradox of stillness is that it often emerges not in withdrawal but in choosing how to engage. A family might agree that the dinner table is a no-device zone, transforming mealtime into an oasis of genuine connection. A workplace might designate a room for silent work, protecting at least part of the day from interruption. In these cases, the sacredness lies in boundaries—the clear signalling that this place, or this time, is set apart from the usual turbulence.

There are tensions, of course. Too rigid a ritual can itself become oppressive, the pursuit of sacred space turning into yet another form of control. Equally, not everyone has access to a quiet home or the resources to carve out architectural sanctuaries. But even here, the principle endures. A person might learn to anchor silence in something as simple as the act of putting on headphones without music, or pausing for breath at the threshold before entering a noisy room. The sacredness lies less in the physicality of the space than in the fidelity of the intention.

What emerges is a reframing of space as psychological technology. Just as we design tools to extend our bodies—glasses to sharpen vision, keyboards to amplify thought—we can design spaces to extend our minds, protecting them from intrusion and guiding them toward clarity. But this requires vigilance. In a world where every corner threatens to be colonised by notifications and noise, the act of setting aside even a chair, a corner, or a ritual becomes quietly radical.

The open question is whether these micro-environments are sufficient against the tide of modern distraction. Can a candlelit corner hold its sanctity when a phone buzzes across the room? Can a daily ritual withstand the encroachment of perpetual urgency? Perhaps sacred spaces endure not because they eliminate the noise but because they remind us, however briefly, that another rhythm is possible. They are signals to the self, and to others, that quiet is not a luxury but a discipline worth defending.

The Value of Doing Nothing

In the late nineteenth century, the German philosopher Friedrich Nietzsche warned that modern life was creating what he called a "restless compulsion for work," a ceaseless drive that dulled thought rather than sharpened it. He argued that the capacity for deep reflection, for true creativity, required *Muße*—a German word connoting leisure not as idleness in the pejorative sense, but as spaciousness, the fertile ground from which insight could emerge. More than a century later, the warning feels prophetic. In an age that glorifies productivity, the simple act of doing nothing is regarded as wasteful, even shameful, despite growing evidence that it may be the very condition for clarity and innovation.

The paradox is striking. Never before have human beings been able to outsource so many tasks to machines, yet never before have they been so busy. Emails, calendars, instant messages, and endless streams of content ensure that few moments pass unfilled. "Dead time" has become an enemy to be conquered. Waiting for a train? Scroll. Standing in a queue? Check emails. The cracks in the day that once invited daydreaming or silent observation are now patched with stimulation. What gets lost is not merely rest, but the mind's ability to wander, to process, to recombine fragments of experience into something new.

Neuroscience is clear: idleness is not inactivity. When the brain is not engaged in focused tasks, the so-called *default mode network* lights up—a constellation of regions involved in autobiographical memory, imagination, and perspective-taking. This network is most active when we are daydreaming, reflecting, or drifting in thought. In other words, doing nothing is the brain's laboratory for meaning-making. Artists, scientists, and innovators have long intuited this. The chemist August Kekulé famously conceived the structure of the benzene ring not at his desk but in a reverie, imagining a snake seizing its own tail. Moments of apparent "laziness" are often crucibles of discovery.

Yet the cultural suspicion of stillness runs deep. The Protestant work ethic, industrialisation, and contemporary hustle culture have conspired to equate worth with output.

Idleness has been recast as weakness. Even leisure is repackaged as productivity: fitness regimes to optimise performance, holidays framed as opportunities for "recharging" before returning to work at greater intensity. In this worldview, rest is not valued for itself but tolerated only as a tool for future efficiency. What disappears is the radical notion that unstructured time has intrinsic worth—that a human being may simply *be,* not continually *do*.

Consider the psychological consequences of this denial. The constant demand for productivity feeds anxiety: every pause feels like falling behind. Over time, the nervous system adapts to relentless stimulation, becoming uncomfortable in silence. Studies show that many people now prefer receiving small electric shocks to sitting alone with their thoughts for fifteen minutes. This is not simply a curiosity; it reveals a profound alienation from the rhythms of the self. Without intervals of quiet, mental chatter grows louder, emotional regulation falters, and decision-making becomes reactive rather than reflective.

But when idleness is reclaimed, its benefits are immediate and far-reaching. Creative professionals often report breakthroughs occurring in the shower, on walks, or while gazing out of a window. These moments, far from trivial, allow the brain to shuffle the deck of memory and association, generating connections that structured effort alone could never produce. Psychologists note that regular "white space" in a schedule fosters not only originality but resilience, giving the mind opportunities to reset its emotional balance. Far from being indulgent, doing nothing becomes a discipline that underwrites sustained clarity.

Practically, this discipline requires courage. In cultures that reward constant motion, carving out emptiness feels transgressive. It may involve deliberately scheduling unstructured time into the day, protecting it as fiercely as one would a meeting. It may mean resisting the urge to fill small interstices with screens—allowing the mind to drift while commuting, waiting, or resting between tasks. It may even involve embracing boredom, recognising that what begins as discomfort often ripens into insight.

Historical and cross-cultural traditions confirm this truth. Monastic practices across Buddhism, Christianity, and Sufism have long understood silence and stillness not as absence but as presence—a gateway to clarity. The Japanese concept of *ma* celebrates the pause, the space between notes in music or brushstrokes in art, as essential to meaning. These traditions remind us that doing nothing is not an abdication but an active stance: the cultivation of receptivity, the willingness to meet the world without agenda.

The resistance, however, is not easily overcome. Many fear that in doing nothing, they will confront thoughts they have been avoiding. Idleness strips away distraction and exposes the raw material of the self. Yet it is precisely in this confrontation that emotional regulation deepens. Neuroscientific studies suggest that unstructured time allows the amygdala, the brain's threat detector, to recalibrate, reducing overreaction to daily stressors. By pausing, by stepping back from constant striving, one learns to meet inner turbulence with perspective.

The deeper question, then, is not whether we *can* afford to do nothing, but whether we can afford not to. A culture without stillness breeds minds that are perpetually busy yet rarely clear, endlessly active yet inwardly exhausted. Rehabilitating idleness requires a reframing: from wastefulness to wisdom, from passivity to a quiet form of mastery. Doing nothing is not an escape from life but a return to it—an invitation for creativity, clarity, and balance to arise in their own time.

And perhaps the true challenge lies here: what would it mean to live in a way that honours stillness not as a temporary relief but as an integral part of being human? To allow ourselves not just fleeting interludes of emptiness but to weave idleness into the very fabric of a meaningful life? The question remains open, and in that openness lies its power.

Silence as a Social Signal

In 1968, during a presidential debate in the United States, there was a moment when neither candidate spoke. The moderator had posed a difficult question, and rather than rushing to fill the space with words, one candidate paused, held the silence, and let the weight of reflection show on his face. Commentators later observed that it was not the eventual answer that won him approval, but the pause itself: the signal that he was listening inwardly, considering carefully, resisting the urge to perform. Silence, in that instant, spoke louder than speech.

Such moments are rare in public life. We inhabit a world that prizes verbal fluency, quick responses, and constant commentary. To hesitate is often seen as weakness; to leave silence in a conversation is perceived as awkward. Yet this cultural suspicion of silence blinds us to its subtle power.

Quiet can be more than an absence of noise: it can function as a social act, shaping relationships, opening spaces for empathy, and signalling respect in ways words cannot.

In Japanese culture, this is formalised in the concept of *ma*—the meaningful pause. In many African traditions, elders allow silence to stretch before answering a question, communicating that wisdom takes time to ripen. Even in Western psychotherapy, clinicians are trained to let silence linger, trusting that in those gaps patients often disclose truths that hurried words might conceal. Silence is not emptiness but presence; it communicates attentiveness, containment, and sometimes even love.

The science of conversation supports this. Studies in interpersonal communication show that people tend to fill silences of more than two seconds, often with superficial or self-protective speech. Yet when one participant resists the impulse, the quality of dialogue deepens. Listeners report feeling more heard when their words are followed by reflective silence rather than immediate response. The pause communicates: *your words matter enough to deserve digestion*. Neuroimaging suggests that such moments allow for deeper processing of emotional cues, fostering empathy and reducing defensiveness.

Of course, silence can also wound. In families, the "silent treatment" is often a form of withdrawal, a refusal to engage that generates isolation rather than intimacy. In professional settings, a manager's prolonged silence after a presentation may induce panic, interpreted as judgement rather than contemplation. The challenge, then, is to discern intent. Silence as connection differs profoundly from silence as punishment. One builds trust; the other corrodes it.

This duality reveals silence as a form of language, one with its own grammar. Just as tone can transform the meaning of words, context shapes the meaning of silence. A pause after a heartfelt disclosure can affirm: *I am with you*. A pause after a mistake can signal patience, or disdain. In this sense, silence demands a literacy of its own—a capacity to read not only words but the spaces between them.

Philosophically, silence disrupts the modern obsession with performance. We are conditioned to prove competence through speech, to occupy space with opinions, to demonstrate value by constant contribution. Choosing silence resists this cultural script. It says: presence need not always be proved. It reclaims conversation as mutual exploration rather than competitive display. The paradox is that silence, often feared as weakness, can embody strength—the confidence to hold space without rushing to control it.

Practical application is possible in everyday life. In negotiation, strategic silence often elicits concessions, as the other party seeks to relieve the tension by speaking first. In teaching, allowing a question to hang in the air invites students to think more deeply, rather than offering surface answers. In friendship, pausing before replying can prevent reactive defensiveness, creating room for genuine understanding. These are not mere techniques but expressions of a deeper orientation: a willingness to value depth over speed, presence over performance.

Still, silence requires courage, particularly in cultures that equate it with discomfort. It asks us to resist the reflexive urge to respond, to let go of the illusion that words alone sustain relationships. This courage is cultivated through practice: deliberately pausing in meetings, letting a loved one finish fully before answering, or even experimenting with shared silence during a walk or meal. In such spaces, connection is not diminished but heightened.

And yet, one cannot ignore the unease silence brings. Why is it so threatening? Perhaps because it reveals vulnerability—our longing to be understood, our fear of being judged, our discomfort with the unknown. To sit in silence with another is to confront these realities together. It requires trust. But precisely in that trust lies its transformative potential.

What if our most powerful form of communication was not our capacity to speak, but our willingness to be quiet? What if true intimacy, in both personal and professional life, depended less on the words we craft than on the silences we honour? The answer may not be comfortable, but it lingers—like silence itself—waiting to be felt as much as understood.

Chapter 11
Listening for What Matters

On the morning of his Nobel lecture, the physicist Richard Feynman recalled a childhood memory that had little to do with quantum mechanics. He described walking with his father, who pointed at a bird and asked not *what* it was called, but *what it was doing*. Anyone could recite a name, his father explained, but it took a different kind of attention to notice the tilt of the head, the rhythm of the wings, the shift in behaviour that revealed a hidden truth. It was a lesson in distinguishing signal from noise: the surface chatter of labels versus the deeper information life offers when we learn how to listen.

Our minds are filled with birds of their own—snatches of thought, fragments of memory, flares of emotion—all fluttering at once. Some of these are mere echoes, the repetitive self-commentary that fills our days without adding meaning. Others carry genuine information: an emotion signalling a neglected need, an intuition pointing towards risk or opportunity, a memory tugging us back to a forgotten value. The challenge is not that we lack inner voices, but that we struggle to tell which ones matter.

This difficulty is amplified by modern culture. The endless feed of external noise—from news cycles to social media scrolls—conditions us to mistake immediacy for importance. We become hyper-responsive to the loudest signals, whether they come from outside or within, while missing the subtler cues that actually shape our well-being. The result is a paradox: the more connected we are, the less attuned we become.

Yet the mind, when quieted, is capable of remarkable discernment. Neuroscience has begun to show what contemplative traditions long intuited: that emotions are not distractions but data, that self-awareness allows for more skilful choices, and that the stories we tell ourselves about our lives can either imprison or liberate us. To learn to listen inwardly is not to indulge in endless introspection, but to cultivate a radar for what is true, relevant, and aligned.

In this chapter, we will examine how to separate signal from noise in the landscape of thought; how to treat emotions not as interruptions but as information worth decoding; how to anchor decisions in the compass of our deepest values rather than the pull of passing chatter; and how to re-author our narratives in ways that are both honest and empowering, avoiding the emptiness of borrowed affirmations.

The stakes could not be higher. For the quality of our listening—what we choose to attend to, and what we allow to fall away—determines not only how we feel but how we live. To listen for what matters is to refuse to be ruled by the loudest voice, whether external or internal. It is to discover that clarity is not the absence of noise but the art of discerning amidst it. The question that remains is simple, and demanding: when your own mind is speaking, can you tell when it is telling the truth?

Signal vs. Noise

One of the most famous innovations in twentieth-century science was not a new machine, but a distinction. In 1948, Claude Shannon published *A Mathematical Theory of Communication,* in which he described the problem of separating *signal*—the meaningful transmission of information—from *noise*—the interference that distorts or obscures it. Though Shannon's concern was the fidelity of telephones and radio systems, his insight reaches far beyond engineering. Human consciousness itself can be understood through this lens: our inner world is flooded with inputs, but only a fraction carries genuine meaning. The rest is static.

We have all known the exhaustion of mistaking noise for signal. A student rereads an email draft twenty times, unable to send it for fear of imagined offence. A parent lies awake at 3 a.m., replaying a throwaway comment from a colleague as if it were an indictment. An executive, presented with clear evidence of success, instead fixates on the single critical remark in an otherwise glowing review. In each case, the mind generates loops of chatter, but beneath them lies something more valuable: an unmet need for reassurance, a longing for belonging, or a reminder of one's vulnerability. The art is in discerning which thoughts are static and which are information.

Modern neuroscience provides a stark reminder of why this is so difficult. The brain's default mode network—active when the mind is not focused on external tasks—tends to produce repetitive, self-referential content. This evolutionary design served an ancient purpose: scanning for threats, rehearsing social interactions, preparing for potential conflict. In the modern environment, however, the same circuitry amplifies rumination. Left unchecked, the brain privileges noise, because noise feels urgent, even when it is irrelevant.

The task, then, is not to silence the inner world, but to tune it. Like a radio operator filtering out static, we must learn to distinguish between the repetitive loops of self-criticism and the quieter but more authentic signals that reveal values, needs, or insights. A recurring thought of "I'm failing" may be noise if it merely replays anxiety without basis. But if it points to a neglected responsibility or signals misalignment between one's work and one's principles, it carries the weight of signal. The difference lies not in the volume of the thought, but in its truthfulness.

Consider the practice of cognitive behavioural therapy (CBT). At its core, CBT trains individuals to test their thoughts against evidence. The process itself is an exercise in separating signal from noise: asking whether a catastrophic prediction is supported by fact, or whether it is simply the brain's static at full volume. This method demonstrates that discernment is not only psychological but epistemic—an ongoing interrogation of what the mind claims as true.

Yet there is tension here. If one treats every thought as disposable noise, one risks missing the faint signals that guide growth. Dreams dismissed as impractical may actually point towards suppressed creativity. A gnawing sense of unease in a relationship may signal boundaries being crossed, even when words have not yet been spoken. Philosophers from Kierkegaard to Simone Weil have warned against ignoring the subtle inner murmurs that hint at our deepest commitments. The challenge is not to disbelieve the mind wholesale, but to cultivate a discriminating ear.

Practical strategies emerge when we hold this tension in view. Mindfulness practices, for example, do not demand that one accept every thought as signal; they create the space to observe without immediate reaction, revealing which patterns dissipate and which persist with significance. Journalling can serve a similar purpose: on paper, repetitive noise often reveals itself in circular phrasing, while genuine signal sharpens into clarity. Even bodily cues—the quickened heart, the tightened chest—can help us notice when an inner voice is echoing fear rather than insight.

The metaphor of signal and noise also reframes how we approach emotions. Anger replayed in endless mental rehearsals is often noise, yet the original flare of anger may have been signal: a boundary crossed, an injustice endured. Sadness that becomes habitual despair may be noise, while sadness that points to grief or to the absence of meaning is signal worth heeding. In this sense, emotions are not enemies to be silenced but messengers to be decoded.

Seen in this light, discerning signal from noise is both a technical and a moral skill. It is technical because it can be trained, with tools drawn from psychology, philosophy, and contemplative practice. It is moral because it demands that we live truthfully: that we neither dismiss every thought as trivial nor cling to every passing chatter as revelation. It requires the courage to ignore what is loud but empty, and the humility to attend to what is quiet but essential.

The question is not whether our minds produce noise—they always will. The question is whether we can refine the art of listening so that, amidst the static, we catch the thread of what matters. And here lies the unresolved challenge: in an age where external noise multiplies by the second, can we still trust ourselves to hear the faint signal that points us back to who we are?

Emotion as Information

Imagine a dashboard without gauges. The car moves, the engine hums, but there is no way of knowing whether the tank is empty, the oil pressure is failing, or the engine is overheating. Most of us would never drive in such ignorance; yet many of us move through life in precisely this way, treating our emotions as irrelevant noise rather than essential instruments. Anger, sadness, joy, fear—these are not random sparks of mental activity. They are data. They tell us something about our needs, our values, our safety, and our connections. To dismiss them is to drive blind.

And yet, for centuries, emotion has been cast as the enemy of reason. Philosophers from Plato to Descartes privileged rationality as the higher faculty, relegating emotion to the realm of weakness and error. In the modern workplace, the bias persists: to be "emotional" is to be irrational, unprofessional, unstable. But contemporary neuroscience tells a different story. Antonio Damasio's landmark research with patients who had suffered damage to emotion-processing areas of the brain revealed a startling truth: without access to emotional cues, people could not make even the simplest decisions. They could list pros and cons indefinitely, but remained paralysed. Rationality, it turns out, requires feeling. Emotion is not a distraction from intelligence but its partner.

Take fear. At its core, fear is an evolutionary signal of threat. It prepares the body to act—heart racing, muscles tightening, senses sharpening. But in modern contexts, fear often misfires. A fear of public speaking may not signal physical danger, but a fear of social judgement. The key is interpretation: is the fear data about a real, imminent threat, or is it noise, a relic of overactive circuitry? In one case, the body is wisely warning; in the other, it is echoing an outdated script. The task is not to suppress fear, but to decode it.

Anger offers another illustration. Dismissed as destructive, anger is in fact an indicator of violated boundaries or perceived injustice. A society that teaches its citizens to bottle anger risks losing the very signals that drive reform and protect dignity. The problem lies not in anger's existence but in its handling: does it become an uncontrolled outburst, or does it guide constructive action? To recognise anger as data is to see beyond its heat and trace it back to the underlying value it defends.

Sadness, too, carries meaning. When someone withdraws after loss, their sadness is not a malfunction; it is a recalibration, urging reflection, rest, and connection with others. Recent research suggests that sadness sharpens memory and promotes more careful, accurate thinking. It is the mind's way of slowing us down to process reality. By contrast, ignoring or stigmatising sadness leads to secondary suffering: the shame of feeling low, layered on top of grief itself. Here again, the data is in the message—

something of value has been lost—and attending to it helps us live more honestly.

Even joy, often celebrated uncritically, deserves examination. Joy points us toward what matters most, but it can also mislead when tethered to fleeting rewards. The high of social media validation, for example, may feel like joy, but often it is the dopamine rush of approval rather than a deeper fulfilment. The discipline lies in distinguishing surface-level gratification from the signal of genuine alignment with one's values.

Philosophically, to treat emotions as information shifts the terms of our relationship with ourselves. Instead of judging feelings as good or bad, we begin to ask: *What is this emotion trying to tell me?* Anxiety may be a warning that one is overextended, or it may simply be static from a perfectionist inner critic. Curiosity and discernment are required to tell the difference. Like a scientist examining data, we must look for patterns, context, and corroborating evidence before drawing conclusions.

Practical strategies follow naturally from this orientation. One is labelling: research by Matthew Lieberman and colleagues has shown that simply naming an emotion reduces its intensity and makes it easier to manage. Another is journalling, which allows emotional "data" to be externalised, analysed, and placed in context. A third is mindfulness, which helps us notice emotions as passing experiences without being hijacked by them, enabling us to attend to the message without drowning in the messenger.

Yet, there is a tension here worth acknowledging. If we over-intellectualise emotions, we risk flattening them into mere codes to be cracked, stripping them of their immediacy and depth. A parent's grief at losing a child is not just "data" about love; it is a lived reality that defies abstraction. Emotions are both information and experience. To treat them only as signals risks dehumanising ourselves; to treat them only as raw feelings risks being swept away by them. The art lies in holding both truths: emotions as messengers, and emotions as part of what it means to be alive.

To live wisely, then, is not to silence our feelings but to learn their language. They will sometimes exaggerate, sometimes mislead, sometimes cry wolf. But they will also whisper truths that reason alone cannot reach. The open question is whether we are willing to listen—not with gullibility, not with hostility, but with the respect due to a compass pointing us, however shakily, toward what matters.

The Inner Compass

How do we know what to do when the map runs out? In a world overflowing with data, opinions, and obligations, decision-making often feels less like a confident step forward and more like stumbling through static. Yet there is a paradox: the most important decisions—whether to leave a job, pursue a relationship, or change a life direction—rarely yield to spreadsheets or pro–con lists alone. Instead, people often speak of "gut instinct" or "something inside me knew." This isn't mysticism; it is the operation of an inner compass, a faculty born of metacognition, clarity, and the quieting of noise.

Consider the contrast. A surgeon in the midst of a complex procedure cannot pause to tally every variable; a musician improvising in front of an audience cannot calculate every note. Their mastery emerges from deep familiarity with their craft, but also from their ability to sense when the body, mind, and context align. Neuroscientists suggest this alignment comes when the prefrontal cortex—the seat of self-monitoring and reflective awareness—works in harmony with older emotional and intuitive systems. Metacognition, the ability to observe one's own thinking, enables them to steer rather than be dragged by impulse. In such moments, decision-making becomes less about reacting and more about choosing in accord with inner signals.

Modern culture, however, rewards speed and external validation. The demand to be always responsive—to emails, metrics, markets—creates a climate in which we confuse urgency with importance. Choices are made in the fog of constant stimulation, where the loudest voice wins, not the wisest. This is why cultivating stillness is more than a luxury; it is a prerequisite for alignment. The inner compass cannot be consulted in a storm. Only when mental chatter subsides does its needle settle enough to reveal direction.

The idea that clarity emerges from quiet is not new. In the Stoic tradition, Marcus Aurelius wrote of withdrawing into "the little field within," a retreat not of place but of mind. In Buddhist practice, mindfulness offers a method of noticing thoughts without clinging, revealing beneath the noise a subtler layer of intention and value. Even in secular cognitive science, researchers describe metacognitive pauses as critical "decision checkpoints"—moments where one recognises bias, recalibrates priorities, and avoids the traps of impulsive reasoning. Across cultures, the wisdom converges: those who cultivate awareness of their own mind make choices that are more resilient, more authentic, and less prone to regret.

Yet the compass metaphor deserves scrutiny. Unlike an external compass, which always points north, the inner compass is not infallible. It can be distorted by unresolved trauma, internalised cultural scripts, or unexamined fears. A person who has always been taught that self-worth depends on achievement may "feel" compelled to overwork, mistaking conditioning for truth. Here metacognition plays its corrective role. To notice not only the thought—*I must succeed*—but the structure of the thought—*Where did this rule come from? Do I still accept it?*—is to disentangle noise from guidance. The compass, in other words, must be calibrated.

Calibration comes through practice. Techniques like journalling, mindfulness meditation, or Socratic questioning all serve to create distance between stimulus and decision, enabling us to hear the deeper signal beneath transient noise. Over time, this strengthens what psychologists call "self-concordant goals"—choices aligned with intrinsic values rather than external pressures. Studies suggest that pursuing such goals predicts greater persistence, satisfaction, and wellbeing. In practical terms: when a decision aligns with one's core values, it feels lighter to carry, even if it is difficult.

But the inner compass is not only about personal fulfilment; it has ethical weight. Decisions ripple outward. A leader who has quieted their inner noise is less likely to be swayed by ego or fear, more likely to choose in ways that serve both self and others. Conversely, leaders trapped in reactive patterns amplify noise on a collective scale—corporate cultures of burnout, political climates of polarisation. The alignment of an individual mind can, in subtle ways, recalibrate an entire community.

Still, a lingering tension remains. If the inner compass is so crucial, why do so many ignore it? Perhaps because listening inward often delivers uncomfortable truths. The compass may point away from comfort, prestige, or convention, toward risk or loss. It may reveal that the role we've invested in no longer fits, or that the relationship we cling to must end. Silence clears the static, but it also removes excuses. And so the question becomes: do we want clarity, or the illusion of safety that noise provides?

To cultivate an inner compass, then, is not merely to make better decisions. It is to accept responsibility for seeing clearly, and for acting in accordance with what is seen. The mind, once quiet, does not leave us in peace; it asks us to live in truth. Whether we heed that call or turn back into distraction is the choice that defines not only what we do, but who we become.

From Noise to Narrative

Every mind carries a story. Some are explicit, rehearsed in words and memories; others hum beneath awareness, shaping emotion and behaviour without ever being spoken aloud. A paradox lies at the heart of human consciousness: the very narrative that gives coherence to our lives can also become the cage that confines us. When our inner story tilts towards inadequacy, catastrophe, or self-blame, it magnifies mental noise into a relentless echo chamber. Yet when re-authored with clarity and truth, narrative does not silence reality but reframes it, transforming noise into signal.

Consider the life of Viktor Frankl, the Austrian psychiatrist imprisoned in Nazi concentration camps. In the bleakest of circumstances, he noticed that survival often hinged less on physical strength than on narrative orientation. Those who could anchor their suffering within a story of meaning—whether love, faith, or purpose—were more resilient than those who could not. Frankl did not claim that story erased suffering, but that it altered its weight. This illustrates the essence of re-authoring: we cannot control every fact of life, but we can reshape the frame in which those facts reside.

The danger, however, is to mistake narrative reframing for empty affirmation. Telling oneself *I am enough* without examining the structures of belief beneath it risks creating another layer of noise. Cognitive behavioural therapy warns of this pitfall: simply replacing one untested thought with another does little to shift entrenched patterns. A person convinced they are unworthy does not become resilient through repetition of a phrase, but through evidence-based reappraisal—by collecting lived experiences that contradict their distorted self-assessment, and then weaving these moments into a revised story.

Modern neuroscience supports this distinction. Functional MRI studies show that when individuals reinterpret a negative experience—asking what can be learned, or what alternative explanations exist—the prefrontal cortex exerts top-down regulation on the amygdala, dampening emotional reactivity. The story we tell ourselves literally rewires the circuits of stress and perception. The same research shows that superficial positive affirmations, when incongruent with self-belief, can heighten distress rather than relieve it. The lesson is clear: narrative healing depends on truthfulness, not slogans.

Yet truthfulness does not mean brutal self-criticism. Language matters. The phrase *I failed at this task* carries a different weight than *I am a failure.* The first identifies an event; the second cements an identity. Narrative re-authoring begins with precision of language, disentangling behaviour from essence, circumstance from destiny. It involves asking: What actually happened? What interpretation am I layering on top? Which story constrains me, and which story liberates me without denying reality?

Examples abound. A student who misses an exam might initially adopt a catastrophic narrative: *This proves I am irresponsible; my career is ruined.* With guidance, they can reframe: *This event reveals I need to manage time differently; one setback does not define me.* The facts remain unchanged, yet the narrative shifts from fatalism to agency. Similarly, an entrepreneur whose venture collapses may tell themselves *I am not cut out for this,* but reframing allows: *This attempt has taught me skills and resilience I could not have gained otherwise.* Such reframings are not delusions; they are deliberate acts of perspective that allow forward movement rather than paralysis.

The philosophical stakes are profound. Human beings are narrative creatures, not merely biological machines. We seek coherence, even in chaos. Myths, histories, personal journals—all testify to our need to organise experience into story. But the question is whether the story we carry is one we have consciously authored, or one written for us by circumstance, culture, or early conditioning. To reclaim authorship is to shift from being a passive character in one's life to being, at least in part, the narrator.

Still, narrative re-authoring carries tension. How do we balance self-compassion with accountability? If we rewrite every failure as a triumph, we risk delusion. If we dwell only on mistakes, we court despair. The art lies in balance—acknowledging wounds without being defined by them, extracting meaning without falsifying facts. A re-authored narrative must remain anchored in truth, yet oriented toward growth. It is less about telling a prettier story than about telling a fuller one.

In practical terms, this can be cultivated through reflective practices: writing exercises that trace recurring inner scripts, mindfulness techniques that expose thought patterns as transient events, or dialogues with trusted others who act as co-editors of our stories. Each method introduces distance between the self and the script, allowing revision rather than blind recitation. Over time, the once-unquestioned narrative softens, revealing alternative interpretations and new chapters waiting to be written.

Yet perhaps the deepest question is this: if narrative is so powerful, can we ever know what is "true," or are we always spinning stories? The answer may lie not in discarding narrative but in cultivating awareness of its plasticity. The mind will always narrate; the task is to ensure that its story is both honest and empowering, tethered to reality yet open to possibility. To live without narrative is impossible. To live with an unexamined narrative is dangerous. To re-author with care is to transform noise into a voice that guides rather than haunts.

And so the unresolved challenge lingers: in the silence between thought and reappraisal, when the old story falters but the new one has not yet taken shape, will we have the courage to author differently—or will we allow the noise to write for us?

Chapter 12
Living with a Quieter Mind

It is one of the paradoxes of modern life: never has humanity had more tools to simplify existence, and never has the inner landscape been more crowded. Notifications, obligations, and endless streams of comparison flood the mind until silence feels almost alien, even unsafe. Yet beneath the static lies something most people long for—a steadier rhythm of thought, a mind not frantically pulled but calmly centred. The challenge is not merely to snatch fleeting moments of calm, but to build a way of living where clarity is protected and nourished.

The idea of a quieter mind often evokes stillness in retreat: monks in cloisters, ascetics in deserts, or sages under banyan trees. But history tells another story too. Thinkers, artists, and leaders who lived in the thick of noise—Seneca in the bustle of Rome, Simone Weil in the factories of industrial France, or even athletes performing in arenas filled with thousands—found ways to guard inner quiet not by escape, but by design. The real question is not *whether* it is possible, but *how* one can cultivate and sustain such clarity while moving through the turbulence of everyday life.

This chapter turns from theory to practice, from the "why" of quieting the mind to the "how" of living with it. The focus is not on transient hacks but on durable structures: the design of mental environments, the cultivation of resilient habits, the calibration of work and rest, and the acceptance that quiet is never a final destination but a discipline continually renewed.

Daily life is the true testing ground. Routines, small choices, and environments act either as shields or as amplifiers of mental noise. A phone kept at arm's length during meals, a deliberate ritual before bed, or even the arrangement of a workspace can either preserve cognitive clarity or fracture it. These decisions, often dismissed as trivial, accumulate into atmospheres that shape thought and attention more powerfully than any single moment of willpower. To live with a quieter mind requires not only self-awareness but architectural intent.

Yet clarity cannot mean insulation from chaos. Crises—personal, professional, or collective—will come, often unbidden and without warning. The measure of quiet is not whether panic never arises, but whether trained awareness allows one to meet turbulence without being consumed by it. Neuroscience has begun to confirm what ancient traditions long claimed: practices that cultivate presence recalibrate the nervous system, reducing the reactivity of stress circuits and allowing more deliberate responses. Here, resilience becomes less about control and more about stance—the capacity to be bent without breaking.

Equally vital is the balance between intensity and renewal. Just as muscles strengthen not in exertion but in recovery, so too the mind requires periods of deliberate rest to sustain its sharpest focus. The science of peak performance underscores a rhythm of oscillation: deep work balanced with deep rest. Without this, clarity corrodes into fatigue, and noise returns louder than before. Sleep, play, and intentional pauses are not indulgences but essential disciplines in the architecture of mental quiet.

And finally, there is the recognition that this is never a project completed. Quieting the mind is not a summit at which one arrives, certificate in hand, but a craft refined over a lifetime. Each season of life brings new challenges to clarity—parenthood, ageing, career upheavals, global uncertainty—and with them, new opportunities to practice. The reward is not perfection but trajectory: a gradual turning away from reactivity and towards perspective, from static to signal, from noise to narrative coherence.

What emerges is a vision both humbling and empowering. The quieter mind is not a fragile state to be protected at all costs, but a practice woven into the fabric of living—structured, resilient, rhythmic, and ongoing. The question that remains is not whether you can quiet the noise for an hour or a day, but whether you can build a life in which silence and clarity are not exceptions but companions. The work begins not in theory, but in the choices that follow.

Designing Your Mental Environment

Imagine entering a library where every book has been torn from the shelves and thrown into chaotic piles. Important texts are buried under trivial pamphlets, voices of wisdom drowned by meaningless chatter. It would be almost impossible to think clearly in such a space. Yet for many people, this is how the mind feels: a cluttered environment where signal and noise blur together. The paradox is striking: we spend enormous effort designing our physical surroundings—choosing furniture, arranging workspaces, curating digital devices—yet give far less attention to the architecture of the mental environment in which our attention and clarity depend.

The twentieth-century architect Le Corbusier once observed that "a house is a machine for living in." He meant that the design of physical space shapes human experience. Neuroscience and psychology now show that the same principle applies inwardly: routines, habits, and digital choices form the scaffolding of mental clarity. Left unmanaged, these structures become disordered, creating a life filled with constant interruption, reactive thought, and depleted attention. When designed deliberately, however, they protect space for reflection, foster resilience, and allow the mind to sustain depth in an age addicted to distraction.

Designing a mental environment is not about withdrawing into ascetic minimalism or controlling every second of the day. Rather, it is about recognising that the mind does not operate in a vacuum. The cues of our surroundings, the rituals that bookend our days, and the streams of information we consume shape cognition as powerfully as diet shapes the body. The person who curates their digital intake, guards their focus through ritual, and creates intentional boundaries will not merely think more clearly—they will live more deliberately.

One of the first domains where environment exerts its influence is routine. Researchers in behavioural science repeatedly find that decision fatigue corrodes both clarity and self-control. Each unresolved choice drains cognitive resources, leaving the mind more vulnerable to noise. Structured routines—morning practices that minimise decision-making, set times for exercise, deliberate pauses for reflection—act as anchors in the day. They automate the ordinary so that the extraordinary can receive attention. A leader who begins with journalling rather than scrolling, or who sets a predictable rhythm for deep work, not only clears their schedule but also clears their mind.

Digital design may be the most urgent frontier of mental architecture. The average person checks their phone hundreds of times daily, often not for need but out of habit triggered by cues. Every notification is an intrusion, every algorithmic feed a river of borrowed voices. The philosopher Herbert Simon warned that "a wealth of information creates a poverty of attention," and nowhere is this more evident than in our relationship with screens. Designing a healthier digital environment does not require rejecting technology altogether; it requires intentionality. Silencing non-essential notifications, setting app limits, or creating device-free zones are not small lifestyle tweaks but profound shifts in the ecology of attention.

Equally significant is the cultivation of micro-environments—spaces deliberately marked as quiet zones. This may be a chair reserved for reading, a corner of the room used solely for meditation, or even the ritual of brewing tea before sitting to write. By linking physical cues with states of mind, we train the nervous system to associate environment with clarity. Neuroscience shows that context-dependent memory and behaviour are deeply intertwined: the room in which we act becomes part of the habit itself. Over time, these micro-environments act as shortcuts, leading the mind into stillness without effort.

Yet clarity cannot be maintained through external design alone. Habits are the invisible architecture of the mind. Consider the distinction between reactive habits—checking emails at the slightest vibration—and intentional habits—setting aside two focused intervals to respond with attention. Both are equally habitual, but only one preserves cognitive clarity. The cultivation of protective habits, from mindful pauses between meetings to evening rituals that signal rest, establishes a rhythm that shields against the noise of modern life. Here, habit is not constraint but liberation: it frees the mind from chaos.

The deeper question, however, is philosophical. To design a mental environment is to confront one's values. What voices will you allow to enter? Which rhythms will you prioritise? In an age where productivity is idolised, the refusal to be perpetually available is not laziness but clarity of purpose. To structure life around what matters is an act of self-authorship, a declaration that not every demand deserves a reply and not every noise deserves to be amplified.

There are tensions, of course. Structure can drift into rigidity, and digital restraint into avoidance. A carefully designed environment must allow for flexibility and unpredictability, recognising that clarity grows not from hermetic isolation but from balanced engagement. A parent's routine may collapse under the unpredictability of children, a professional's rituals disrupted by urgent demands. The art lies not in perfect control, but in having resilient structures that can bend without breaking.

Designing your mental environment is, in essence, designing your attention. Attention is the currency with which we purchase our lives, and it is always being spent—whether squandered on noise or invested in depth. The environment determines much of the exchange rate. The real question, then, is whether we are willing to build the mental architecture that protects clarity, or whether we will allow it to be built for us by algorithms, habits of distraction, and the pressures of culture.

If clarity is precious, then its preservation requires more than fleeting intention. It demands design. And design, once undertaken, raises its own quiet challenge: not simply *how* to structure a mental environment, but how to inhabit it wisely. The answer begins not tomorrow, not in some imagined retreat, but in the very next choice—the next routine observed, the next notification silenced, the next space consecrated to attention. In this sense, every day is an act of design, and every act of design is a vote for the kind of mind one will live within.

Resilience in the Face of Chaos

On the morning of 15 January 2009, Captain Chesley "Sully" Sullenberger lifted US Airways Flight 1549 from LaGuardia Airport. Within minutes, a flock of geese disabled both engines. Thousands of feet above New York City, the passengers' lives depended on the next ninety seconds. What followed was not panic but poise. Sully and his co-pilot assessed options, dismissed impossibilities, and landed the plane on the Hudson River, saving all 155 souls aboard. When asked later how he achieved such calm under pressure, Sully replied that decades of training had prepared him to silence inner noise and focus on what mattered most.

The story is dramatic, but the principle is universal. Crises—whether personal, professional, or global—confront us with the unexpected. They compress time, flood us with stimuli, and threaten to overwhelm the mind with static. In those moments, it is not the person with the most information who prevails, but the one who can maintain clarity amidst chaos. Resilience, in its deepest sense, is not toughness or stoicism; it is the trained capacity to respond without being consumed by noise.

At first glance, chaos seems synonymous with disorder. Yet psychologists studying crisis response note a paradox: moments of upheaval are also moments when clarity can emerge with startling sharpness. This is not accidental. The human nervous system, when regulated, is capable of extraordinary focus. The difficulty lies in the fact that untrained awareness is prone to scatter under pressure, amplifying fears and catastrophic predictions. Awareness trained through deliberate practice, however, becomes a stabilising anchor. It allows the individual to discern between noise and signal, to prioritise action over reaction, and to preserve inner equilibrium while others are swept away.

Consider the firefighter entering a burning building. Without cultivated awareness, the mind might spiral into panic: *What if the structure collapses? What if I am too late?* With trained focus, those thoughts are acknowledged but not obeyed. The body moves in line with training, the mind attends to the present task. This is not denial of danger but the disciplined refusal to let noise dictate action. Cognitive neuroscience confirms that mindfulness training enhances activity in the prefrontal cortex—the region governing executive control—while dampening reactivity in the amygdala, the brain's alarm system. Simply put: awareness, when practiced, rewires the mind to face chaos with clarity.

The philosopher Epictetus argued that we cannot control external events, only our responses. Modern psychology echoes this with the concept of *response flexibility*—the ability to insert a pause between stimulus and reaction. In crises, that pause is the difference between rashness and wisdom. But the pause cannot be improvised at will. It is cultivated in ordinary life through micro-practices: noticing the breath before a difficult conversation, observing the body's tension before making a decision, returning attention to the present in moments of restlessness. These seemingly small acts become the reservoir of resilience, drawn upon when the stakes rise.

Yet resilience should not be confused with detachment. To remain clear does not mean to remain unaffected. Soldiers trained in mindfulness-based resilience programmes still feel fear; emergency doctors still feel urgency. What changes is the relationship to those feelings. Instead of being swept into identification—*I am panicking*—they can observe with distance—*panic is present, but I am still choosing.* This shift, subtle yet profound, transforms emotion from master to messenger.

The cultural narratives of resilience often glorify toughness: the stiff upper lip, the unbreakable will. But resilience in the face of chaos is less about resisting vulnerability and more about transforming it. Neuroscience shows that attempts to suppress fear or stress often backfire, heightening arousal. By contrast, acknowledging and naming emotions reduces their intensity. Awareness allows chaos to be metabolised rather than denied, integrated rather than repressed. True resilience is not armour; it is permeability without collapse.

Examples abound in quieter settings. A professional blindsided by sudden redundancy may experience waves of anger, grief, and fear. Without trained awareness, these emotions spiral into self-recrimination and paralysis. With it, the same emotions are recognised as natural responses. They are allowed without domination, creating space for measured decision-making—whether seeking new opportunities, rethinking priorities, or reaching for support. The outer event remains the same; the inner noise is transformed.

There is also a philosophical depth to resilience that extends beyond crisis management. Chaos reveals the limits of control, reminding us of the fragility of plans and the unpredictability of life. To cultivate awareness is, in part, to accept this truth without despair. It is to recognise that certainty is an illusion, but clarity is not. We may not command the storm, but we can learn to stand within it without losing our bearings. The mind trained in awareness becomes not invulnerable, but agile. It bends without breaking.

Still, a tension remains. How do we balance preparedness with openness? Too much structure and we risk rigidity; too little and we risk collapse. The answer may lie in recognising resilience not as a fixed trait but as a living practice. It requires continuous tuning—like a musician adjusting an instrument to remain in harmony despite changing conditions. The crisis may differ in scale or form, but the practice remains the same: returning, noticing, choosing.

The measure of resilience, then, is not how loudly we assert strength in calm waters, but how quietly we act with clarity when the tide turns violent. And yet one question lingers unresolved: in a culture that prizes speed and reactivity, how do we make space to train the very awareness that chaos will one day demand? The answer, like resilience itself, cannot be given once—it must be practised, day after day, until silence in the storm becomes second nature.

Deep Work, Deep Rest

In 1914, Henry Ford made a radical decision that defied the prevailing wisdom of his age. At a time when most industrial labourers worked six days a week for ten or more hours a day, Ford introduced the forty-hour workweek. His reasoning was not moral but practical: exhausted workers made costly mistakes, lost focus, and produced less. To the astonishment of his competitors, productivity at Ford's factories surged. Ford had stumbled on a principle that modern neuroscience, performance psychology, and sleep science now confirm: sustainable excellence requires a rhythm of intense focus and deliberate rest.

The paradox is as relevant to knowledge work as it was to factory floors. In an age of digital distraction, global competition, and the cult of productivity, many professionals push their minds as if they were machines. Yet the brain is not built for unbroken concentration. Research from cognitive science reveals that mental performance follows ultradian rhythms—natural cycles of roughly 90 to 120 minutes of heightened focus followed by a need for recovery. Push through those recovery windows, and output does not simply plateau; it deteriorates. Errors multiply, creativity wanes, and mental noise amplifies.

Psychologist Anders Ericsson's famous studies on elite performers—musicians, athletes, chess grandmasters—uncovered a consistent pattern: those at the very top did not practice more indiscriminately; they practiced in concentrated blocks of "deep work," followed by purposeful rest. The violinists who excelled most were not those who played ten hours a day, but those who practised with full attention for about four, interspersed with recovery and sleep. Excellence, Ericsson concluded, depends less on relentless effort than on the quality of alternation between exertion and renewal.

The modern workplace, however, often punishes rest and glorifies constant busyness. Open-plan offices, endless notifications, and the expectation of 24/7 availability erode the capacity for sustained attention. As a result, many confuse activity with productivity. Yet neuroscientists show that during states of deep rest—especially sleep—the brain consolidates learning, prunes irrelevant connections, and incubates insights. The hippocampus, the brain's memory hub, replays recent experiences during slow-wave sleep, integrating them into long-term knowledge. REM sleep, meanwhile, fosters emotional regulation and creative problem-solving. To forgo rest is not to "gain time" but to impoverish thought itself.

The balance of deep work and deep rest is therefore not merely a lifestyle preference; it is a biological necessity. Consider the work of chronobiologist Till Roenneberg, who has shown that people have distinct circadian profiles—larks, owls, and those in between. Aligning deep work with one's natural peaks in alertness, and honouring valleys with restorative breaks, enhances both performance and well-being. Misalignment, by contrast, leads to what he calls "social jetlag"—a perpetual state of cognitive fatigue that undermines clarity and resilience.

Cultural traditions have long intuited what science now demonstrates. Monastic orders, from Benedictine abbeys to Zen monasteries, structured their days around alternating periods of labour, prayer, and rest. This rhythm was not accidental; it acknowledged the limits of attention and the need for renewal. Modern professionals can borrow from this wisdom, not by retreating to cloisters, but by structuring their days with intentional cadence: blocks of uninterrupted focus shielded from distraction, balanced with deliberate pauses—walks, naps, meditation, or simply moments of stillness.

There is also a philosophical dimension to the discipline of balance. The relentless pursuit of productivity often masks an underlying fear: that worth is measured by output alone. Deep rest challenges this narrative by asserting that value also lies in receptivity—in the mind's ability to absorb, integrate, and rejuvenate. To rest deeply is to trust that silence, idleness, and sleep are not indulgences but essential conditions for clarity and creativity. This reframing is not easy in cultures that equate stillness with laziness, but it is indispensable for those who seek depth rather than speed.

Importantly, rest is not simply the absence of work. Scrolling through social media or binge-watching series may provide temporary distraction but rarely true recovery. Rest that restores clarity is active in its passivity: a mindful walk in nature, time in conversation without agenda, an afternoon nap, or practices of meditation and breathing that reset the nervous system. Neuroscientist Andrew Huberman notes that even short periods of non-sleep deep rest (NSDR), such as yoga nidra, can accelerate recovery and restore focus. These micro-practices, woven into the day, offer counterbalance to the overstimulation of modern life.

Still, tension remains. How does one balance the ambition for achievement with the humility of rest? Push too far into discipline, and rest becomes another item on the to-do list, stripped of its spontaneity. Drift too far into comfort, and focus dissolves into procrastination. The art lies in holding both with equal seriousness: to work deeply when it is time to work, and to rest deeply when it is time to rest. Neither is an escape from the other; each completes the other.

The reward is profound. Those who master this rhythm find not only greater productivity but greater peace. Their days are not fragmented by distraction, nor their nights by restless thought. They enter crises with reserves of clarity and creativity, because they have cultivated cycles of renewal. And yet one question presses forward, unresolved: in a culture that still equates busyness with virtue, who will have the courage to protect both their deepest work and their deepest rest—and to model a different way of living and leading?

The Ongoing Practice

In 490 BCE, the Greek soldier Pheidippides is said to have run from the battlefield of Marathon to Athens, announcing victory before collapsing in exhaustion. His feat of endurance, later mythologised into the modern marathon, has long been a symbol of human perseverance. Yet if his story teaches anything beyond legend, it is this: a single burst of effort, however heroic, is unsustainable. Endurance is built not on moments of extreme exertion but on practices repeated, cultivated, and integrated into daily life. Quieting the inner noise belongs to this same category. It is not a sprint towards serenity but a discipline of ongoing return.

The paradox of inner stillness is that it cannot be "won" once and for all. No matter how clear the mind feels after a retreat, a practice, or even a single moment of deep calm, the world rushes back in—emails arrive, family needs surface, unexpected crises break open the day. The quiet that once felt secure is tested again and again. To imagine calm as a permanent state is to court disappointment; to recognise it as a practice, constantly renewed, is to step into something more durable and realistic.

This understanding reframes mental clarity as less like a possession and more like a craft. The musician does not perfect the violin in one session; the athlete does not master form in one training; the philosopher does not resolve questions in a single conversation. Each returns daily to the work, sharpening skill through repetition. Likewise, cultivating inner quiet requires returning, over and over, to simple yet profound practices: breathing, pausing, reflecting, choosing.

Psychological research supports this view of clarity as a discipline. Studies on neuroplasticity show that repeated attention to practices such as mindfulness, gratitude journaling, or body-based awareness creates lasting changes in brain circuitry. The prefrontal cortex strengthens its regulatory role over the amygdala, allowing emotion to be experienced without spiralling into rumination. Yet these benefits fade when the practice stops. Much like physical fitness, mental clarity diminishes without maintenance. The very fragility of this balance underscores its nature as a lifelong discipline.

There is also a deeper philosophical truth here. Many traditions have grappled with the tension between fleeting calm and enduring transformation. The Stoics spoke of *askēsis*—not a rigid asceticism but a daily exercise of the mind to prepare for fortune's blows. Buddhist teachers describe practice as "beginner's mind," the humility of knowing one must return to stillness freshly each day, without relying on yesterday's insight. Both perspectives converge on a recognition: the work of inner life is never finished, and therein lies its dignity.

In practical terms, sustaining the discipline of quiet requires designing routines that can weather disruption. This does not mean building rigid schedules that collapse when travel, deadlines, or crises intervene. Rather, it means cultivating adaptable anchors: the short morning ritual that grounds the day, the evening reflection that signals closure, the breath practice that can be summoned even in a crowded train or tense meeting. These small, repeatable actions function like keystones, holding the structure of quiet amid the turbulence of daily life.

Equally important is the cultivation of perspective when lapses occur. Everyone abandons their practices at times—missing meditation, skipping rest, letting digital noise spill unchecked. The danger lies not in the lapse itself but in the interpretation: "I've failed; I've lost it." Such self-criticism only amplifies noise. The wiser stance is to see the discipline as forgiving: every lapse is an opportunity to return, and every return strengthens the habit of resilience. What matters is not perfection but persistence.

The metaphor of training is useful here. The runner who misses a week does not lose all endurance; the body remembers, and recovery comes quicker with each cycle. Likewise, the mind remembers quiet. Each time one comes back to silence after noise, the return becomes easier. Neuropsychologist Richard Davidson calls this "emotional style": individuals differ in how quickly they recover from disruption, but with training, resilience improves. The goal is not to eliminate noise altogether—an impossible task—but to shorten the distance between distraction and return.

A roadmap for sustainable practice therefore rests on three pillars. The first is *consistency*: small daily rituals that serve as scaffolding. The second is *adaptability*: the ability to scale practices up or down depending on circumstance. The third is *compassion*: recognising that the discipline is not about unbroken calm but about the courage to return after every interruption. Together, these form not a rigid system but a living rhythm—an art of resilience.

Yet one cannot ignore the tension between discipline and spontaneity. Too much structure risks suffocating the very quiet it seeks to cultivate; too little dissolves into inconsistency. The ongoing practice is thus a negotiation, a conversation with life itself. Some days demand intensity, others gentleness; some call for stillness, others for movement. The skill lies in sensing which is needed—and adjusting without abandoning the larger trajectory.

In this sense, quiet becomes less a goal than a companion. It is something to walk with, to return to, to grow alongside. The noise never vanishes entirely; it recedes and returns, like the tide. But over time, one learns not to fear the tide's return. One learns, instead, to trust the rhythm of coming back. And perhaps the deeper question is not whether we can silence the mind forever, but whether we can build a life where returning to quiet is as natural, and as necessary, as breathing.

Chapter 13
Beyond Silence: The Mind as an Ally

In the winter of 1804, Ludwig van Beethoven faced a crisis. Deafness, the very affliction that should have ended his career, was tightening its grip. The constant ringing in his ears was a torment, a noise so relentless it might have silenced most musicians. And yet, out of this condition came the *Eroica Symphony*—a composition of such daring scope that it redefined the possibilities of music. Beethoven's mind was not quiet. It was turbulent, discordant, unrelenting. But it was not his enemy. He learned to shape the noise, to turn it into something greater.

The paradox is familiar to all of us. The same mind that floods with anxious chatter at night, replaying conversations and forecasting failures, is also the source of our best ideas and our deepest insights. The same restless questioning that keeps us awake can, under a different light, be the spark of invention or the quiet nudge toward truth. Silence, valuable though it is, cannot be the whole story. For if the mind can be stilled into calm, it can also be tuned into resonance. The challenge is not to abolish the noise but to orchestrate it.

Modern psychology and neuroscience increasingly affirm this duality. Daydreaming, once derided as distraction, is now recognised as the brain's "default mode network," a system essential for creative problem-solving and long-range planning. The chatter that feels wasteful is, at times, the compost from which originality grows. Leaders, artists, and thinkers alike have long drawn on this paradox: balancing stillness with thought, contemplation with action, silence with speech. The mind is not an unruly beast to be broken but a complex instrument to be mastered.

This chapter asks what it means to move beyond the binary of noise versus silence, towards a relationship with the mind that is more nuanced, more generous, and more powerful. It will begin by reframing mental chatter as potential—raw, unrefined, and often overwhelming, but capable of being harnessed into insight and creativity. It will then explore the art of integration: how silence and thought can exist in partnership rather than opposition, providing balance and depth to our inner lives.

From here, the lens will widen to the broader implications of mental clarity—not just for individual peace, but for leadership, decision-making, and human connection. In a world awash with distractions and pressures, those who can listen inwardly with precision while maintaining external clarity gain a decisive advantage. The ability to quiet, focus, and then act from a place of alignment is no longer a private luxury but a public necessity.

And finally, the chapter will offer a vision of life in which inner noise, though never gone, no longer rules. Instead, it becomes like background music: sometimes stirring, sometimes fading, always present but never dominating. A life where one can live both audibly and quietly—engaged with the mind's richness without being consumed by it.

The invitation, then, is not to escape the mind but to befriend it. Not to silence its voice but to teach it to harmonise. The question that follows—and that will carry us through these pages—is this: what might it mean, in a noisy world and a restless mind, to discover not merely relief in silence, but an ally in thought?

From Noise to Music

On a rainy afternoon in Princeton in the 1930s, Albert Einstein would often be seen walking alone, his pipe in hand, muttering to himself. Neighbours thought him eccentric, but those rambles, punctuated by seemingly distracted monologues, were the crucible of theory. What looked like restless chatter was in fact a mind circling, reframing, and eventually striking upon insights that altered our understanding of the universe. The noise was not noise at all. It was the overture to music.

We tend to think of mental chatter as the enemy of clarity, an interference pattern distorting the signals we most need to hear. And indeed, when unbridled, it can be paralysing—rumination looping endlessly, anxious rehearsal of imagined futures, the relentless replay of past embarrassments. Yet beneath the apparent chaos lies a paradox: the same internal turbulence that unsettles us can, when directed, become the soil of invention. What distinguishes suffocating noise from fertile hum is not its existence but how it is handled.

Cognitive science has begun to map this paradox in detail. The brain's so-called "default mode network" activates when attention drifts, producing the free associations that are the raw material of creativity. Daydreams, half-formed thoughts, even the inner nagging we often wish to suppress—these are the sparks that, once shaped, can ignite original solutions. The novelist struggling with a plot, the mathematician circling a stubborn theorem, the engineer replaying a design flaw: all rely on a background chatter that is, in truth, the workshop of the imagination.

Still, there is a crucial tension. Not all noise transforms into music. Some of it consumes bandwidth, dragging attention into sterile cul-de-sacs. The challenge, then, is one of cultivation. Just as a composer distinguishes melody from dissonance, we must learn to discern between mental patterns that merit amplification and those that need to fade into silence. Here the disciplines of reflection, mindfulness, and structured practice become essential—not to eliminate thought, but to provide it with form.

Consider the practice of deliberate incubation. Thomas Edison famously kept a steel ball in his hand as he dozed in his chair; when his muscles relaxed, the ball fell and woke him, allowing him to harvest the half-dreamt images of hypnagogia. Modern studies confirm the value of this liminal state: brief periods of rest or wandering attention often precede creative breakthroughs. The noise, when suspended between wakefulness and sleep, is softened into pliable material that the conscious mind can then sculpt.

A more everyday example lies in the rhythm of focused work followed by release. Psychologists studying problem-solving note that intense concentration often leads to an impasse, while stepping away—taking a walk, engaging in mundane chores—allows unconscious processing to continue. What feels like "mental noise" during these intervals is, in fact, the brain quietly recombining elements, testing hypotheses, generating novel configurations. The chatter is less a distraction than a rehearsal.

Yet one must also confront the danger of mistaking repetition for insight. The anxious mind, replaying a slight or rehearsing an argument, often masquerades as productive thought but produces only exhaustion. Here lies the philosophical challenge: how to distinguish signal from illusion, insight from echo. The answer may lie not in silencing the noise, but in adopting a stance of curiosity towards it. To ask: *What is this thought trying to tell me? Is it a creative association, or merely the shadow of fear?*

From a cultural perspective, this reframing is radical. Our age venerates efficiency and linear progress, leaving little tolerance for what looks like meandering thought. But history shows that meandering is often the prerequisite of mastery. Darwin's long walks, Virginia Woolf's stream-of-consciousness drafts, Steve Jobs' insistence on "walking meetings": each is a testament to the productive interplay of chaos and order, chatter and clarity. Noise, properly harnessed, does not slow us down. It prepares us for leaps that focus alone cannot yield.

Philosophically, the movement from noise to music mirrors the human struggle for meaning itself. Life presents us with fragments—impressions, half-memories, conflicting impulses. The task is not to suppress them in pursuit of sterile order but to weave them into coherence. Just as dissonance in music, when resolved, heightens the beauty of harmony, so too does the turbulence of the mind, when integrated, enrich the texture of our inner lives. Silence may offer respite, but noise offers depth.

In practice, this demands both discipline and surrender: discipline to cultivate the mental habits that channel thought, surrender to allow the mind its restless play without immediate judgement. It is in the oscillation between these modes—between structured silence and wandering chatter—that the conditions for originality arise. The question is not whether we can escape the noise, but whether we can learn to listen differently.

If so, the cacophony within us is no longer a foe but a partner, an orchestra tuning before the symphony begins. The unresolved challenge, and the invitation that follows, is this: can we learn not merely to endure our inner chatter, but to compose with it—transforming distraction into melody, restlessness into rhythm, and noise into the music of a life more fully lived?

Integrating Thought and Stillness

In the late evenings, Blaise Pascal would write furiously in fragments, searching for words that might capture the trembling insight of faith and reason. Yet he also confessed that "all of humanity's problems stem from man's inability to sit quietly in a room alone." The paradox is striking: a brilliant mind propelled by restless thought, while simultaneously recognising that without stillness, the very faculty that gave him genius could turn to torment. The same paradox confronts us all.

For centuries, human cultures have oscillated between reverence for silence and celebration of intellect. In monasteries, silence was cultivated as a gateway to the divine. In universities, argument and reasoning were sharpened into tools of civilisation. The question has never been whether silence or thought is superior, but how they might coexist. To privilege one and suppress the other is to distort the human experience; to integrate both is to unlock its fullness.

Modern neuroscience adds a contemporary lens to this ancient tension. Functional brain scans show that the networks responsible for focused attention and those engaged during restful, unfocused awareness are not enemies but partners. The analytical prefrontal cortex thrives in moments of problem-solving, but when allowed to step back, the default mode network orchestrates a quieter form of integration—linking disparate memories, simulating futures, finding meaning in chaos. A mind dominated by constant reasoning burns out; a mind lost in perpetual stillness risks passivity. It is their interplay that creates resilience and depth.

Examples abound in both art and science. Beethoven, deaf and wracked by despair, alternated between long walks in the Viennese woods and intense compositional bursts at his desk. Those walks were not idle retreats but incubators of melody, where stillness seeded new possibilities that disciplined labour could later refine. In a different domain, contemporary research on elite athletes shows that micro-moments of stillness—breath regulation before a free throw, visualisation before a sprint—dramatically enhance performance. Thinking and silence are not opposites here; they are partners in a finely tuned choreography.

The danger lies in mistaking stillness for an escape from thought, or thought for an enemy of inner peace. In truth, both can become tyrannical when unbalanced. Endless rumination suffocates clarity, but a rigid pursuit of silence can become a spiritual bypass, a denial of the mind's generative role. To live wisely requires a posture of alternation: knowing when to let thoughts run, and when to let silence gather them into coherence.

Consider decision-making. The executive who rushes into action without pausing risks reactive choices, driven by bias or urgency. Yet the one who delays indefinitely in meditation risks paralysis, never bringing insight into the world. The most effective leaders practise a rhythm: periods of deliberate thought sharpened by analysis, followed by pauses that allow intuition to surface. Neuroscientists describe this as metacognition—the capacity not merely to think, but to step back and observe thinking itself. In such moments, stillness does not cancel thought; it frames it, refines it, and renders it trustworthy.

Philosophically, this integration resonates with Aristotle's vision of the *golden mean*: virtue lies not at the extremes but in balance. Too much stillness, and life collapses into quietism; too much thinking, and the mind devours itself. Yet balance is not a static point—it is a dynamic, lived practice. Every day requires recalibration. In the quiet of dawn, the mind may rest in silence; in the bustle of work, thought must sharpen and act; in the evening, reflection may weave the two together into meaning.

What makes this integration so vital today is the cultural tilt towards noise—intellectual, digital, and emotional. The 24-hour news cycle, endless notifications, and productivity culture reward constant engagement of thought without the counterbalance of stillness. The result is not only burnout but a narrowing of imagination. Silence, by contrast, expands the field of vision, allowing new connections to emerge. The integration of the two is not a luxury; it is a corrective necessity.

But stillness itself is not merely the absence of thought. It is an active presence, a quality of attention that reframes the mental landscape. In meditation, silence sharpens awareness of the mind's movements, making thought more transparent and less tyrannical. In dialogue, silence between words deepens listening, making thought more responsive and humane. In creativity, silence gives rise to what cannot be forced by will alone. In each case, silence enriches thought, while thought gives silence its shape and application.

The challenge, then, is practical: how to cultivate this interplay in a life that constantly drags us towards imbalance. Some practices are deceptively simple: beginning a meeting with a single minute of quiet before discussion; stepping away from the desk when an argument loops fruitlessly; ending the day not with more input but with stillness to let the day's noise settle into insight. Over time, these micro-disciplines build a rhythm where silence and thought no longer compete, but cooperate.

Ultimately, the integration of thought and stillness is not about restraining one and exalting the other, but about recovering a lost partnership. The mind is at its most luminous when it can move fluidly between the two: silence providing the canvas, thought the brushstrokes; thought sketching possibility, silence revealing proportion. The question that remains for each of us is not whether we can think less or be silent more, but whether we can learn to let each illuminate the other—so that life itself becomes richer, not by subtraction, but by harmony.

Clarity as a Leadership Skill

During the Cuban Missile Crisis in October 1962, the world stood a breath away from nuclear catastrophe. In the pressure cooker of those thirteen days, both John F. Kennedy and Nikita Khrushchev were surrounded by advisers demanding action, hawks urging escalation, and a relentless flood of intelligence reports that blurred more than they clarified. What prevented disaster was not superior firepower or the volume of information available, but the ability to quiet inner panic, sift through noise, and act with clarity. In that crucible, the capacity to think clearly under extreme pressure was not merely a personal advantage—it became a skill that shaped the fate of millions.

Leadership, at its core, is an exercise in discernment under uncertainty. Yet today's leaders face a peculiar paradox: access to unprecedented amounts of data, yet increasing difficulty in distilling it into insight. The external noise of constant communication is matched by an internal chorus of doubts, biases, and imagined scenarios. In this environment, clarity is no longer optional—it is a discipline, and for those who aspire to lead well, a defining skill.

The misconception is that clarity emerges naturally from intelligence or experience. In practice, it is cultivated. A leader might possess encyclopaedic knowledge or brilliant analytical ability, but if their inner world is saturated with distraction and self-doubt, decisions will be distorted. Neuroscience underscores this point: the prefrontal cortex, responsible for reasoning and executive function, is particularly vulnerable to emotional overload. When stress or mental clutter floods the system, rational thought narrows, and tunnel vision takes over. The leader who cannot quiet this inner static risks mistaking noise for signal.

Clarity begins with self-awareness. The Stoics understood this when they taught that mastery of one's perceptions precedes mastery of events. Modern performance psychology echoes the same lesson. Elite athletes, when faced with moments of immense pressure, rely on techniques to regulate inner chatter—breathing routines, reframing thoughts, narrowing attention to the immediate task. Leaders, though rarely trained in this way, face similar demands. The boardroom may not resemble a football pitch, but the stakes of distraction are just as high.

Examples of this abound in contemporary leadership. Consider Satya Nadella's transformation of Microsoft. His emphasis on cultivating a "growth mindset" was not just a cultural slogan; it was a reframing of the company's inner narrative. By shifting away from defensiveness and internal competition, Nadella fostered clarity about what mattered: innovation and empathy for users. The external results—renewed relevance, stronger partnerships, soaring valuation—were built upon a quieter, clearer internal foundation.

Clarity also reshapes relationships. A leader's presence radiates far beyond their words. When inner noise dominates—when impatience, insecurity, or unchecked ego colours interactions—teams respond with guardedness and confusion. Conversely, a leader who listens fully, pauses before reacting, and speaks from a place of composure creates psychological safety. Research in organisational behaviour consistently shows that teams led by such individuals not only perform better but also experience greater trust and cohesion. The silence a leader carries within becomes contagious, enabling others to lower their own inner noise.

Yet the cultivation of clarity demands more than momentary techniques. It requires a structural commitment to practices that guard against overwhelm. Many leaders, ironically, sabotage themselves by filling every hour with meetings, emails, and reactive tasks—leaving no space for reflective thought. The most effective ones deliberately carve out silence: walking without devices, scheduling time for deep work, or starting the day with meditation. These practices are not indulgences but necessities, ensuring that when crises arise, the mind is not already saturated with static.

Philosophically, clarity as a leadership skill raises a deeper question: is it simply a tool for efficiency, or a quality of character? The best leaders demonstrate that it is both. It allows for sharper strategy, but it also anchors integrity. When inner noise is quieted, values can surface more clearly. Decisions then align not just with expediency but with principle. In this sense, clarity is as much ethical as it is cognitive.

The tension, of course, is that no leader operates in perfect silence. Pressure, politics, and personal fears will always create noise. The discipline lies not in eliminating it, but in recognising it for what it is and refusing to be ruled by it. In moments of uncertainty, clarity does not guarantee perfect outcomes. What it guarantees is a steadier hand, a sharper perception, and a capacity to act with coherence rather than confusion.

The lesson is as urgent now as it was in the missile crisis: clarity is not simply an inner luxury; it is a form of leadership capital. In a noisy age, those who can cultivate stillness within are better equipped to navigate the turbulence without. The unresolved question—the one each aspiring leader must ask—is whether clarity will be left to chance, or whether it will be pursued deliberately, as a discipline as vital as strategy or communication. For in the end, the leader's greatest asset is not only their vision of the world, but the quietness of mind that allows them to see it clearly.

Living Audibly and Quietly

There is a peculiar liberation in standing at the edge of a concert hall when the orchestra has finished. For a moment, the silence is not empty but full—resonant with echoes of what has just been played. The music no longer demands attention, yet its presence lingers as a subtle undertone. Life, when lived with mastery over inner noise, can feel much the same: thoughts, emotions, and narratives continue to exist, but they no longer command the stage. They fade into background music, leaving space for deliberate, intentional presence.

The paradox is striking. We often imagine peace as the eradication of noise, as if the only path to clarity is a mind emptied of sound. Yet the mind is not built for perpetual silence. Thought is its instrument, chatter its constant rehearsal. The art is not to banish it but to tune it, to live in such a way that the noise becomes accompaniment rather than interference. When this shift occurs, what once seemed oppressive becomes usable. Mental static transforms into melody.

Consider the example of writers, scientists, or composers who report their greatest breakthroughs not in moments of complete stillness, but in the hum of thought gently guided towards form. Albert Einstein admitted that many of his insights came not from intense calculation but from letting his mind wander playfully with images and analogies. Virginia Woolf spoke of the "waves" of consciousness as the material of literature itself. These individuals did not conquer inner chatter by silencing it; they reframed it, hearing within the noise a rhythm that could be shaped into something meaningful.

This vision applies far beyond art or science. In everyday life, the parent managing competing demands, the leader steering a team, or the individual navigating a difficult relationship all face torrents of mental commentary. When taken literally and unexamined, that commentary breeds anxiety and paralysis. But when held lightly—acknowledged, contextualised, and placed in the background—it becomes a subtle guide. Like a musician following the bass line rather than the cacophony of scattered notes, one begins to move with greater coherence.

The philosophical implications are profound. To live audibly and quietly is to recognise that our inner world need not be an adversary. For centuries, spiritual traditions have warned against identification with thought: Buddhism's teaching of non-attachment, Christian mysticism's call to "the cloud of unknowing," Stoicism's focus on perception. Modern neuroscience complements this wisdom, showing how practices such as mindfulness reshape the brain's default mode network, reducing rumination and increasing cognitive flexibility. Yet all of these insights converge on a common truth: the goal is not the annihilation of thought, but the cultivation of right relationship to it.

There is also an ethical dimension. A mind dominated by noise is reactive, self-absorbed, and prone to distortion. A quieter mind, one in which noise has been contextualised, is capable of deeper listening, empathy, and discernment. To live audibly and quietly is not only to liberate oneself from inner chaos but also to engage others with greater presence. Conversations cease to be competitions of who speaks loudest; they become shared spaces where silence itself communicates attention and respect.

Practical life offers countless opportunities to embody this balance. Choosing to pause before answering an email, taking a walk without headphones, or ending the day with a few minutes of reflection are not trivial acts—they are exercises in recalibration. Each one affirms that noise is not sovereign, that the individual can decide when to step into the foreground and when to let it recede. Over time, such choices accumulate, producing a life marked not by constant reaction but by deliberate response.

Yet the tension remains: how does one remain audible in a world that rewards noise? To live audibly and quietly is not to withdraw into monastic silence or passive detachment. It is to participate fully in the conversation of life—speaking, acting, creating—while no longer being enslaved by the inner chorus. It is to make room for both intensity and stillness, knowing that each has its place. The noise becomes music not by being silenced, but by being integrated into a broader harmony.

What emerges is a vision of existence neither dominated by chatter nor sterilised of it. A life in which one can attend to the world's demands without losing the thread of inner stillness. A life where thought supports rather than suffocates, where silence enriches rather than empties. A life audibly engaged, quietly grounded.

And perhaps the question that lingers is this: if the mind is destined always to make noise, what composition will you allow it to play? Will it remain an untuned cacophony, or will you learn to hear in its restless hum the beginning of a score worth living by?

About the Author

Lina Chaen writes about the intersections of mind, culture, and human resilience. Raised in East Asia and later immersed in global communities, she brings a cross-cultural sensitivity to the timeless struggle with overthinking and mental restlessness. Her work draws from cognitive psychology, mindfulness traditions, and lived experience to make complex ideas accessible without diluting their depth. Lina is committed to helping readers cultivate inner clarity in an age of constant distraction, offering practices that are both practical and profound. Her writing is known for its precision, warmth, and ability to make readers feel both understood and equipped to change.

www.ingramcontent.com/pod-product-compliance
Lightning Source LLC
Chambersburg PA
CBHW031342230926
51848CB00002B/354
* 9 7 8 9 3 7 4 1 2 7 4 8 3 *